W9-BOM-602

Praise for

DEFYING LIMITS

"Dave Williams is a Canadian hero. As a distinguished Canadian astronaut, he was part of an elite core of individuals who had both the courage and the privilege to turn their dreams into reality. Through Dave's story, we can all be inspired to set goals, overcome obstacles, and, with hard work and determination, know that we can make a difference."

—RICK HANSEN

"In *Defying Limits*, Dave describes how his passion for aviation and medicine set him on the path to becoming a Canadian astronaut. . . . Dave's humility, teamwork, leadership, and operational skill prove that he has the right stuff. I'd fly with him again anytime."

—SCOTT KELLY, author of *Endurance*

"An inspirational tale of a remarkable Canadian doctor, astronaut, spacewalker, aquanaut, CEO, and loving father who turned failure into astounding accomplishments in space and on the ground. A fabulous example of how to live life to the fullest."

—BOB MCDONALD, CBC's chief science correspondent
and host of *Quirks & Quarks*

"Riveting, inspiring words from a man who has the right, bright stuff. It's all here, from his pitch-perfect pursuit of becoming a physician and astronaut to the perilous, peerless moments during three space walks when wonder captures his heart like love. This is a bracingly informative portrait about exploration, discovery, and what makes life worth living."

—DR. JOE MACINNIS, author of *Deep Leadership*

"Every astronaut is deeply affected by the experience of viewing Earth from space, but how do you share that feeling with others who will never be there? Canadian astronaut Dave Williams uses his most brilliant moments in space—floating alone, anchored only by a tether—to remind himself, and us, to cherish every moment here on Earth. Very few of us can be astronauts, but we can all do that."

—JAY INGRAM, bestselling author of the Science of Why series

DEFYING LIMITS

Lessons from the Edge of the Universe

DR. DAVE WILLIAMS

Published by Simon & Schuster
New York London Toronto Sydney New Delhi

SIMON &
SCHUSTER
CANADA

Simon & Schuster Canada
A Division of Simon & Schuster, Inc.
166 King Street East, Suite 300
Toronto, Ontario M5A 1J3

This Simon & Schuster Canada edition October 2018

SIMON & SCHUSTER CANADA and colophon are
trademarks of Simon & Schuster, Inc.

For information about special discounts for bulk purchases,
please contact Simon & Schuster Special Sales at 1-800-268-3216
or CustomerService@simonandschuster.ca.

Library and Archives Canada Cataloguing in Publication

Williams, Dafydd, 1954–, author
   Defying limits: lessons from the edge of the universe / Dave Williams.
   Issued in print and electronic formats.
   ISBN 978-1-5011-6095-0 (hardcover).—ISBN 978-1-5011-6096-7 (ebook)
   1. Williams, Dafydd, 1954–. 2. Astronauts—Canada—Biography.
3. Physicians—Canada—Biography. 4. Autobiographies. I. Title.
   TL789.85.W55A3 2018   629.450092   C2018-902312-0
                                                 C2018-902313-9

Interior design by Lewelin Polanco

Manufactured in Canada

10 9 8 7 6 5 4 3 2 1

ISBN 978-1-5011-6095-0
ISBN 978-1-5011-6096-7 (ebook)

This book is dedicated to those who aspire to lead happy, fulfilled lives. Time is our most precious resource, not to be squandered but to be nourished into rich experiences that will stay with us forever.

CONTENTS

CONTENTS

PROLOGUE

A Lifetime in a Moment

Time is infinite. Our lives are not. We all know this and the older we get, the more we feel it. As a child, time was something I never really thought about. Days seemed to last forever, filled with continuous activity and new experiences. As I got older, time didn't change, but I did. Days, months, years, whirled by in a flurry of activity. It's so easy to become complacent. But moments can last forever, if we remember to pay attention to them.

Ted Rosenthal, the late poet and author, put it best when confronted in his thirties with his imminent death: "You can live a lifetime in a moment." A lifetime in a moment. That means an hour, a day, a conversation, or an encounter can be as rich and fulfilling as an entire lifetime, but only if we're mindful and self-aware enough to truly embrace the gift of every second we spend on this earth.

I first heard Ted's message years ago when I was in medical school. At the time, I thought I fully understood it. Since then, I've always tried to live my life to the fullest. But it wasn't until much later, when I was outside the space shuttle *Endeavour* during my second space walk, that I *lived* Ted's words. In that moment I understood what Ted meant. It was a moment that will stay with me forever.

It was August 8, 2007. I embarked upon STS-118 as a mission specialist aboard the space shuttle *Endeavour*. This was my second voyage into space, but that didn't make it any easier. This was after the tragic loss of seven crew members on the *Columbia* in 2003, when the shuttle disintegrated during reentry. Those men and women were incredible astronauts. They were also my friends.

The night before my departure, I said good-bye to my wife, Cathy, and my two amazing kids.

"So I'll see you in two weeks?" Cathy said to me as she kissed me.

"Looking forward to it," I replied. We both understood the risks of this trip.

Finally, the moment of the launch arrived. I was ready. With launch preparations completed, I was strapped into the shuttle with my crewmates, and the final countdown was rapidly nearing completion. "Three, two, one, zero. We have ignition, and liftoff."

The crackling boom of the solid rocket boosters was followed by a blinding flash. The raw power threw me back and forth against my restraining harness, and my body was thrust back as we rocketed into the sky. I'd felt it all once before, but that didn't matter. Every time was new. The bouncing and shaking eventually subsided, and a few minutes later I saw the checklists floating around me. I turned to my fellow mission specialists, Barb Morgan and Al Drew, and flashed a thumbs-up.

The trip to reach space lasted only a few minutes, but we still had a two-day journey ahead of us to get to the International Space Station (ISS). During that time, we inspected the orbiter tiles and prepared for our rendezvous, but the real work began after we docked.

On August 13, six days into our trip, it was time to complete one of the primary goals of the mission: a space walk to replace a faulty gyroscope on the space station. Although I didn't know it then, by the end of the trip I would log more than seventeen hours of spacewalking, achieving a new Canadian record. But I didn't care about records. What I cared about was making sure we got the job done and were able to return to the station without issue.

On this walk I was accompanied by one of my crewmates, Rick Mastracchio. It's no small task to leave the relative safety of the space station, remove damaged equipment, and install a brand-new 1,200-pound gyroscope in the vacuum of space. To make it over to the shuttle—which was docked to the U.S. lab at the center of the station—I rode on the end of the Canadarm2. Charlie Hobaugh, who went by his call sign "Scorch," was our pilot. He had the job of controlling the robotic arm. With precision rivaling that of a neurosurgeon, he moved me from one part of the space station to another, down to the payload bay of the space shuttle, and back to the station.

Rick and I made it out of the station airlock successfully and removed the failed gyroscope together. Teamwork is always critical for success. The next step was to install the new gyroscope, a task that required a complex choreography between the robotic arm and the two of us.

Mission specialist Tracy Caldwell was watching our progress from the station's flight deck window and calling out the checklist procedures.

"Tethers configured properly?"

"Roger," I responded. "I'm attached to the gyroscope. I've removed my local tether."

"Copy," Tracy replied.

I started slowly moving in space, anchored only by the foot restraint on the end of the Canadarm2, carefully holding on to the 1,200-pound gyroscope. If my grip slipped or I lost control, the mass of the gyroscope could pull me out of my foot restraint. That would mean two freely floating objects in space—me and the gyroscope. Either of us could collide with the station or shuttle. That was not a scenario anyone wanted.

"Ready for motion," I said to Scorch, meaning I was ready for him to guide me and the gyroscope back to the station. Though I *said* I was ready for motion, actually I felt growing concerns about holding this enormous piece of equipment with two hands, secured only by my feet, which were attached to the end of a robotic arm on a space station traveling at 17,500 miles per hour. But that's what astronauts spend years training for.

Scorch must have sensed my unease. "Dave, just remember: this is not a jettison task." His wry sense of humor was well-known among us. Despite the stress of not wanting to make a mistake, I was grinning from ear to ear underneath my reflective space helmet.

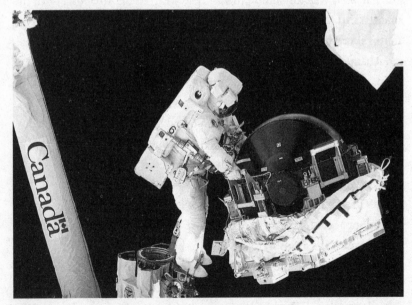

Anchored to the end of the Canadarm2 with a new gyroscope. It was a memorable ride during the six hour, twenty-eight-minute space walk. *Photo courtesy of NASA*

The Canadarm2 began to move, pulling me away from the shuttle's payload bay and back toward the station. At that moment I was fully focused on gripping with my hands and feet. Everything was going according to plan.

Halfway through my ride, Scorch had a question for me. "How's the view out there?" he asked. Leave it to Scorch to ask a question like that. The giant spherical gyroscope was right in front of me, occupying my entire field of vision.

"I've got a face full of gyroscope right now, Scorch. I can't see anything else."

But the truth is, earlier on the journey to the payload bay, I did get my chance to take in the view. And it was spectacular—life altering, in fact. I will never forget the amazing epiphany of looking down and seeing our 4.5 billion-year-old planet, a beautiful blue oasis, cast against the endless black expanse of outer space.

There it was: my home; home to us all. The entire history of humanity had taken place on the planet beneath me. Minus my crewmates, everyone I cared about was down there. Everything that had ever happened to me had taken place there. From my distant vantage point, there were no boundaries evident, no divisions between countries, only majestic continents surrounded by deep-blue oceans.

It was then that I finally understood what it means to live a lifetime in a moment, to appreciate every second you've lived and every second you still have to live. I was filled with gratitude for everything—for my life, for my friends and family, for the chance to see what only a few others had seen before. In that instant it reinforced for me Ted's message: there is no better way to defy the limits of time than by living in the moment. It's a lesson for all of us to live our lives to the fullest while we can, to embrace the richness of our experiences, to stop wondering what our legacy will be and instead live it right now.

PART ONE

1

To Fly in Outer Space

I wasn't born wanting to be an astronaut—but almost. On May 5, 1961, eleven days before my seventh birthday, my parents, sister, and I gathered around the small, grainy black-and-white TV in the living room to watch the CBS news coverage of Alan Shepard's launch from Cape Canaveral, Florida, on the first suborbital flight. The voice of Walter Cronkite, who would later be thought of by many as the voice of the sixties, took us through the final stages of the countdown.

"At T-minus thirty-five, you'll hear the conductor pushing the button on the console and the automatic sequencer takes over," Cronkite said, emphasizing every syllable.

No one really knew what to expect, as many of the launch tests leading up to the flight of *Freedom 7* had ended catastrophically. T-10 seconds and counting down . . . "We have liftoff," fellow astronaut Deke Slayton, the capsule communicator (CapCom), said, the roar of the rocket filling our living room, followed by "We are reading you loud and clear."

I was in awe, completely captured in this moment. It's amazing, looking back at this event now, to think that a fifteen-minute suborbital flight inspired me to pursue a career that seemed almost impossible. But it was real. Perhaps I could do this. Maybe I could be an astronaut and fly to outer space. In my youthful enthusiasm, I managed to overlook the fact that there was no such thing as a Canadian astronaut. Why get bogged down in details when you're nearly seven and Alan Shepard's *Freedom 7* space capsule is floating on-screen in front of you, and you've got your entire life to figure out how you're going to get from terra firma to zero gravity?

"Mom, Dad, can you imagine what it would be like to be up there, to fly in space? Can I do that when I grow up?" A look passed between them.

"It'd be pretty amazing," Dad said. "But I don't think Canada has an astronaut program."

I was a very lucky kid. I had the perfect childhood and I was permitted to daydream about outer space. I was born in Saskatoon, but my father, a bank manager, was transferred to Montréal when I was a year and a half old, and that's where I spent my early years. This was Montréal in the 1960s, very different from the Montréal of today. Our house was on the western end of the island, in the town of Beaconsfield, which is now a major suburb. But back then it was a blend of summer lakefront properties and local farms. Our newly constructed subdivision was an outcropping of a few houses on a dirt road. On one side of our housing development was a farm, and on the other was an apple orchard.

Things were different back then. Like most of the other kids in the neighborhood, we were encouraged to explore freely, to go outside and play rather than stay inside and get in our parents' way. My friends; my older sister, Bronwen; and I spent a lot of time exploring the woods and streams around our house. We used to build rafts and launch them downstream, seeing how far they would carry us before breaking apart and sinking. We would go fishing, or we'd build campfires in clearings in the woods. It was very much something out of *The Adventures of Tom Sawyer*. The only things that were missing were hobo sticks with blanket bundles dangling at the end.

I think back fondly on this time in my life. It's when I first learned about independence and resilience, about relying on myself and my group of friends to make things happen—and how to stay safe. When you're a ten-year-old kid building fires in the woods and playing in streams, it's up to you and your pals to figure out the important things, like how to avoid falling in the stream when it's cold, and how to start a fire without burning yourself or the entire forest down. We used to cook beans and wieners in a can on the fire, then share them. I can still taste the smoky maple flavor and remember the feeling of independence. We were explorers discovering a frontier all our own. I've had many excellent meals since then, but few linger in my memory quite as sweetly as the ones we cooked in the woods.

It's funny how this relates to a question I'm so often asked now: "When does astronaut training start?" Astronaut training starts when you make up your mind that you want to be an astronaut. If you're seven years old, that's when your training starts—in the woods with your pals, learning how to open a can and cook for yourself over a fire.

Not all of my time was spent outdoors, though. Occasionally, I played inside, usually when there was something new to play with or when the weather was so bad that we were forced to stay inside. In the early 1960s my parents bought a brand-new washer and dryer, which in those days was a big deal. Families saved up for these kinds of purchases, and they often marked a big change in lifestyle, especially when the matriarch of the house—in this case, my mother—had the difficult task of keeping two rambunctious kids clean. The appliances arrived in giant boxes, the biggest I'd ever seen. Mom and Dad weren't so interested in the packaging, but my sister and I were.

"Can we have them?" we asked my dad.

"Have what, the boxes?"

"Yes! Yes!"

"Of course," he said. "Do whatever you like with them; just don't make a mess." I ran to the kitchen to grab the serrated knife, perfect for bread but even better for cardboard. "Be careful!" Mom said. "Don't cut yourself."

We quickly got to work and made a "computer" out of one of the boxes. This was no ordinary computer: it was a computer-fort that we could fit inside. We created buttons and knobs, dials and doors, and we even added a little string for the dog to pull to automatically release treats. When I look back, I can't help but notice the types of machines we were emulating and how ultimately I would end up working with the real things as an adult.

In the mid-sixties, by the time I was about ten, my parents actively encouraged a lot of practical skills in me and my sister. One Christmas I got a chemistry set. Another year I got a Phillips electronic engineer kit with a real circuit board! This wasn't a toy you simply stuck batteries in to make it work, though. It was something you had to *make* work by following circuit diagrams. You'd put the wiring diagram on top of a background board with rows of little holes in it that let you hook up the wires, resistors and capacitors, and if you did it perfectly, the thing worked; if you screwed up, no go. The first thing I tried to build was an AM radio, because I wanted to listen to the Beatles after bedtime. It was pretty exciting when I turned it on after lights out and hid under the covers to hear "Twist and Shout" blaring loud and clear.

I went from being a kid captivated by an electronics kit to a graduate student in a neurophysiology lab, where I worked with electronic equipment every day. As a grad student, I had to build some of the

For Christmas in 1962, I got a ChemCraft kit. The skills I learned from that gift made me want to learn more about science.

electronic equipment I needed for my experiments. At McGill University, I was studying the effects of steroid hormones on the brain to understand why patients with overactive or underactive adrenal glands have associated behavioral changes. To do so, I built a device that dispensed hormones in picoliter quantities into the brains of rats. There was no kit for that, only a circuit diagram that I found in an article in the biomedical literature. What prepared me to build this device, and repair some of the other equipment in the lab, was that electronics kit I'd been given as a kid.

I'm sure my parents never imagined the transformative power of one little gift, but somehow, with just about everything, they nurtured my curiosity and sense of discovery. They knew when to let us kids run wild and when to call us back home, when to offer help and when to let us experience the profound effects of failure for ourselves, trusting we'd learn and grow from it. Success feels really good, doesn't it? But I've always found failure to be more instructive. My parents didn't only believe that—they instilled it, and in so doing they laid the groundwork for one of the most important lessons I needed to know in order to become an astronaut. And for that, Mom and Dad, I'll always be grateful.

2

In Your Own Backyard

Exploration begins in your own backyard. Most astronauts know this intuitively. So did my parents. Now that I'm a parent myself, I'm amazed at the courage my mom and dad must have had to let my sister and I do all sorts of crazy things—sometimes with their watchful eyes on us, but often all on our own. I can recall several times when my friends and I would do something stupid in the woods beyond our house or our wild, adventurous plans wouldn't work out the way we hoped. We'd hobble back home, and one of us—okay, occasionally me—would be clutching a bleeding extremity. Fortunately, I never broke anything, but it wasn't for a lack of opportunity! It's easy now to forget all the slips, slides, scrapes, and bumps, but those were as much a part of the journey of exploration as anything else.

As I got older, my machine-building projects went from cardboard computers to a whole new level. I was already learning how to problem-solve and engineer things to make them work. The big thing at the time was to make a minibike, which my friends and I tried to do using a bicycle and a lawn mower engine. My next-door neighbor's father was an engineer, and he showed us how we could mount a lawn mower engine onto a bicycle to motorize it. "It's not that hard," he said. "Just need a bit of power, and a little ingenuity can't hurt, either." He winked at us, then hooked a pulley and belt to the rear wheel of the bike. Rev up the lawn mower, and off you go—no pedaling required!

Needless to say, I decided to modify my own bike the same way. I used my paper route money to buy an old lawn mower and tried to do it myself. It seemed pretty cool, but there was just one problem. A lawn mower has a carburetor, and a carburetor is designed to work when the lawnmower lies flat against the lawn, not on its side against a bicycle. As soon as a carburetor is turned on its side, gravity works against it. This meant I had to figure out a way to modify the carburetor to work sideways so that my minibike would be motor powered, making pedaling a thing of the past. Necessity, as they say, is the mother of all invention.

Somewhere in the process of testing and mounting the engine, I started it without it being attached to the bike frame, preferring a makeshift wooden test stand. Of course, a poorly restrained engine is not particularly safe. The engine fell over and the rotating flywheel caught the top of my left index finger. Initially, I was stunned, but then it started to hurt! With blood streaming from my finger, I went into the kitchen and was greeted with a stern look from my mother. I figured I was in for a visit to the doctor; I'd never had stitches, but I expected it was time for a new experience.

Before my mother had children, she had been an operating room nurse. Blood didn't faze her and she took all of my childhood injuries in stride. If she'd been born today, there's no doubt that she'd train to be a surgeon. But back then female surgeons were beyond rare, and it was an uphill battle for women to move into the higher ranks of the medical establishment. Even though Mom dreamed of a world where she could be more, she loved her work—so much so that her enthusiasm was infectious.

My mother calmly assessed the situation. "No stitches required," she said, reaching for the first aid kit, which was always kept fully stocked and within easy reach. "But next time try to be a little more careful." Mom bandaged and splinted my finger herself. I still have the scar on my finger, a memory of a great day.

When I was about ten years old, Mom decided to teach me how to give an injection. My father suffered from pernicious anemia linked to a deficiency in vitamin B12, and the treatment was monthly injections. "You never know; if I'm not around, you may have to give the injections to him," she announced, grabbing an orange from the fruit bowl and taking out syringes and swabs, which she carefully laid on the spotless kitchen table.

"Cool!" I said, reaching for the syringes, only to get a finger wagged in my face.

"Step one, wash your hands—properly. Meaning with soap and hot water. For at least a minute."

"Right."

Protocols had to be followed. There was no skipping the tedious parts, all of which instilled in me a patience for the process—and for the payoff when things were done right. Mom delighted in turning her kitchen table into a lab. She got my sister and me beakers and flasks, chemicals and condensers, a stethoscope and a microscope. We'd sit together and scour the CENCO (Central Scientific Company) catalogue, then drive to an actual store to pick up our goods, because it was much more fun than waiting for the package to arrive in the mail. One of the many things she ordered for us was a dissecting kit, which she proceeded to teach us how to use.

"Sorry," I'd tell my friends. "Can't ride bikes after school because Mom is teaching us how to dissect." This precipitated a wave of curiosity among my friends. My sister and I dissected dead earthworms that we found lying on the road after a rainstorm. When we went fishing and brought home what we caught, the poor fish were also dissected prior to being cooked and eaten. CENCO also had an array of prepared specimens for purchase and we bought a number of those creatures, including a frog "fixed" in formaldehyde, which we happily dissected. "Anatomy is amazing," Mom would say. "There's so much to be learned."

A few weeks later, one of my friends called. "Hey, Dave," he said. "My mom went to the butcher shop and brought home a beef heart. What do you think? Should we?" Out came the dissecting kit, except this time we really didn't know what we were looking at, so a quick consult with Mom helped me understand why there are four chambers in the heart, what the cardiac valves do and what their names are. Despite the ready availability of the TV and other distractions, this was more exciting than any toy we could have played with. In my mind's eye, I can still picture the muscles of that cow heart and how they worked to pull valves open and closed. Its design was wondrous and enthralling.

When you're a kid, so much is unknown. So much is controlled by the adult world, so much is beyond your reckoning and understanding, so many things are out of bounds. But Mom invited me to the table of adulthood. By the time I was twelve, she was teaching me how to tie surgical knots and talked to me at length about the amazing things that surgeons were able to do to repair the human body. She encouraged me to study how the body functioned, to explore its inner workings, to discover the mechanisms and mysteries of science. And, you know, in moments when she explored with me, I didn't feel like a little kid anymore. On the contrary: I felt like a scientist.

Then there was my father. If I got the exploration gene from anybody, it was from him. Originally from Wales, he was a mountaineer.

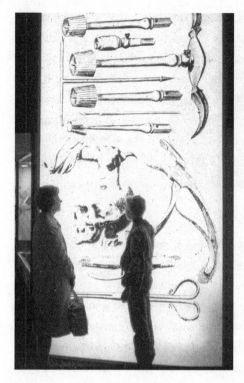

My mom always encouraged me to learn as much as I could about the human body. Here, we're looking at a neurosurgical drawing at Expo '67 in Montréal.

As a young man, he spent a lot of the time climbing and alpine skiing in Western Canada. Today we'd call it heli-skiing, but in those days if you wanted to ski down mountains, you had to climb up on your own with sealskin covers on your skis that stopped you from sliding backward. No fancy helicopters. No chairlifts. No specialized lightweight equipment. To get to the top of the mountain required serious work and skill—all that just to go down once and start at the bottom again.

Dad would climb for the challenge and sheer pleasure of testing his skills to the limit. He summited many peaks, most with names I've forgotten, and there is one photo of him in silhouette sitting on a peak, holding his ice ax and looking off into the horizon.

As a young boy, I'd stare at that photo hanging on the wall: the blue skies, the puffy clouds, and the infinite horizon of mountains—and my dad in the middle of it all. Years later, when I saw the Rockies firsthand, my mind went back to that photo. It captured the essence of exploration, the quest to explore beyond the horizon.

When I was young, Dad used to tell me stories about his climbing days, but they didn't mean much to me then. As Dad grew up, he

My dad, resting at the summit of Mount Shuksan, which he'd just climbed. I'll always be grateful that he passed his love of exploration on to me.

separated himself from his love for the sport. When you're a kid and you're listening to your parents, sometimes you fail to read the significance of what they're actually trying to tell you, only to figure it out later—sometimes too late. Dad was a very proud Welshman and, characteristic of his generation, would rarely share his emotions. What I'd give to ask him now about all his adventures: how he achieved summits with only the most rudimentary gear, what drove him to start at the bottom, and what kept him wanting to climb to the top. I never knew my dad as a mountaineer, only as a bank manager. It took me years to figure out that he'd given up some of his dreams and passions to raise his family—to raise me.

Dad's fascination with aviation was a natural precursor to his passion for human spaceflight. He never let go of his love of outer space. He was obsessed with it—especially with the space program. He had a reel-to-reel tape recorder, and he recorded every television program he could about space travel. To this day, I have tapes of the *Apollo 11* lunar landing with Walter Cronkite narrating. The phrase "And that's the way it is" made space exploration seem achievable for me. If that was the way it was for Neil Armstrong and Buzz Aldrin when they landed on the moon on July 20, 1969, maybe that was the way it could be for me.

Because he was an explorer at heart, Dad understood my wanderlust. When I was a kid, Sunday nights were always the same: dinner, followed by watching *The Undersea World of Jacques Cousteau*, then bath time. I loved Jacques Cousteau. I'd be glued to the screen for the entire sixty minutes. I was amazed by the black-and-white TV images of the serene undersea world set against the infinite gray void of the ocean. *There's the coral, and there are all the fish, but what else is hidden in the gray mist of the underwater horizon?* I wondered.

After watching the show, I'd don my face mask and engage in snorkel exploration of the six-inch depths of the bathtub. The visibility in the soapy water, particularly with the accumulated dirt of a weekend exploring the woods, made it impossible to see much. But in my own mind, I was exploring an uncharted reef on some undiscovered atoll.

My first exposure to the undersea world came from watching the TV show *Sea Hunt*, in which Lloyd Bridges played a U.S. Navy diver. And then the film *Thunderball* came out, showing James Bond in all those cool underwater scenes. All these events in the world of diving captured my imagination, and while I was still supremely interested in space, it seemed that as a Canadian kid my chances of exploring space were nonexistent.

"So you're really sure that Canada doesn't have any astronauts?" I asked my dad, for about the thousandth time.

"I'm afraid not, son."

"Will we *ever* have any Canadian astronauts?"

"I don't know. I hope so. I think so. I think it's possible. Canadian aerospace engineers are among the best in the world. After all, they designed the Avro Arrow and some of those engineers are now working at NASA. Maybe one day we'll have Canadian astronauts."

Prophetic words.

If I couldn't explore outer space, inner space would have to do.

"Dad, I want to learn to dive."

Pause. Deliberation. "Okay," he said. "That sounds good to me."

My collection of space trading cards had broadened to include copies of *Skin Diver* magazine and clippings from *National Geographic* of the Canadian diving doctor Joe MacInnis. I would save the fifty cents from my paper route money to buy each issue. It doesn't sound like much, but that was the equivalent of ten packs of bubble gum—and that was a big deal.

Soon after I pronounced my interest in diving, Dad bought me a diving watch, and one for himself, too. His was a Rolex Submariner like the one James Bond wore in *Thunderball*. Then, in 1967, when I was twelve, he enrolled me in scuba lessons. If you're thinking that sounds a little young for someone to learn to scuba dive, you're right, especially then. The only way I made it into the class was because my father negotiated with the instructor on my behalf.

Dad clarified to me the rules of engagement. "You're going to be the youngest in the class—by far—and probably the smallest, too. The instructors aren't thrilled to have you there. But they will let you try . . . on one condition."

"What's that?"

"You have to do *everything* they say and pass all the tests the adults do. And if not, you don't get your certification. Got it?"

I did. I got it. More than that: I was thrilled! Dad was presenting me with a big challenge and a huge responsibility. He clarified the dangers at length. If I screwed up, if I didn't listen, or if I made a careless mistake, there was the risk that I could get decompression sickness and really bad things could happen to me. I could actually die.

"Okay," I assured him. "I'll do everything I'm told."

"Good. And one more thing," he said. "I'm attending the course with you."

So my father was there for everything. During all the poolside sessions, he sat in the stands and watched. Throughout all the lectures, he sat at a desk nearby and took notes. At home, after the first class, he handed me a binder.

"What's this?" I asked.

"Your class notes. So you can study." He'd typed up notes for me, all of them clearly organized and written in language a kid could understand. He did this after *every* class until that binder was full.

The final exam was one of the biggest challenges of my life. I used all of Dad's notes and committed to studying exhaustively, which would have shocked my elementary school teachers. The written part of the exam covered the mixed-gas laws, the physics of diving, Dalton's law of partial pressures, and decompression tables, but the second I was done, I felt pretty good about it. The pool part of the exam was a significant test of strength and endurance, requiring me to show that I was capable of safely getting in and out of the water with a heavy tank on my back, a weight belt, and all the other diving gear. There were three underwater stations on the bottom of the pool, which was fifteen feet deep. Each station was separated to create a thirty-foot triangle. At the first station, I had to take off my tank and weight belt, then hold my breath and swim to the second station, where another tank that I could breathe from awaited. Then I had to take off my mask and fins, tuck them under the equipment, and swim to the third station to breathe from another tank—this time without my face mask on. After demonstrating I could breathe from a tank without wearing a face mask, I had to swim back to the first station and put on my tank, weight belt, mask, and fins, which the instructor had brought over from the second station. This whole regimen had to be completed without going to the surface for air.

My hard work and studying paid off. Shortly after my thirteenth birthday, I became a NAUI (National Association of Underwater Instructors) certified diver and nine years later a NAUI instructor.

When I wasn't scheming and dreaming about life aquatic, I was looking up into the sky, fascinated by aeronautics and all things related to aviation. Just like Dad. He had been born before the first airplanes were made. He'd witnessed steam engines become diesels, then witnessed trains surpassed by planes, and then the birth of commercial aviation and the first human spaceflights.

We as a family were very fortunate to go on a couple of vacations to Florida. Other people drove, but Dad insisted on flying. He didn't make a lot of money, but he made enough to save up and give us the gift of flight. I'll never forget it—my first time on a plane. It was an Eastern Airlines Boeing 707. I would later come to learn that, like the military version, the NASA Boeing 707 was called the KC-135, also affectionately known as the "Vomit Comet" because of its use in our NASA training. When it flies a parabolic arc in the sky similar to the hill on a roller coaster, it creates brief periods of microgravity where everyone—except the pilots—floats freely in the cabin for twenty seconds. After literally falling out of the sky, this rapid descent transitions into a steep climb during which everyone is exposed to slightly more than twice the force of gravity. This can result in pretty significant motion sickness, so much so that those prone to vomiting often begin to feel queasy when they start walking toward the airplane.

But I didn't know anything about vomit comets back then. Flight travel was calm and civilized—so civilized that we all dressed in our best clothes for the flight. Mom even made sure my hair was combed back neatly, quite uncharacteristic for me. I remember walking out on the tarmac and climbing up the stairs into the plane, a feeling of complete awe overcoming me. I'd packed all my skin-diving equipment into my luggage so that after my voyage into the air I could plunge into the depths of the Florida waters. My gear was such cheap stuff, but I had no idea at the time. To me, it was precious. Once we touched down, I didn't waste any time before I was swimming into the waves and searching the ocean floor for the creatures I had read about in Cousteau's *Silent World*.

Another early and memorable flight experience was when Dad took our family to the Montréal Saint-Hubert Airport to watch the Golden Hawks fly in the Air Force Day air show on June 11, 1960. The

Golden Hawks were the Royal Canadian Air Force aerobatic flying team. From 1959 to 1964, they performed hundreds of shows a year with an eight-plane formation, and in 1960, they were commanded by Fern Villeneuve. They were eventually disbanded but later became the Golden Centennaires that flew at Expo '67 to celebrate Canada's centennial year, and later still, they became the Snowbirds.

I was spellbound watching six of the gold F-86 Sabre aircraft in perfect formation while the two other pilots weaved around their colleague's planes.

"You see that?" Dad said, pointing up so high.

"A CF-101 Voodoo!"

"Yes, that's right."

"And a CF-104 Starfighter, too!"

"You got it."

I'm not sure who was more excited by the show, me or him. Dad gave me a pamphlet he'd received that day, commemorating the Golden Hawks and their amazing feats.

"Could be worth something one day, this Golden Hawks booklet. Why don't you keep it?"

And I did. In 1998, as part of the STS-90 mission, I took Dad's Golden Hawks pamphlet on board the space shuttle *Columbia* for my very first flight into space.

The combination of this early exposure to high-performance aircraft and the exploits of the Mercury astronauts solidified my interest in aviation and aerospace exploration. In grade four, when asked to draw something for an art project, I used crayons to create an image of an aircraft flying over my own unique version of the Golden Gate Bridge, with the sun setting in the background. My friends and I played with balsa wood gliders and had innumerable contests to see whose glider would go the farthest. I decided to add jet propulsion to my glider using a small firecracker. I cut the fuse end off to create a solid-propellant rocket. I carefully taped the firecracker turned rocket engine to the balsa wood. When I lit the firecracker, the glider did in fact take off quickly, but just as quickly it burned up in a big fireball. So much for my future as an aerospace engineer.

From these inauspicious beginnings, I went on to build a number of plastic airplane models, none of which were capable of flight. Then one day in Ted's Hobby Shop, I found a balsa wood model of a Piper Cub, a high-wing, single-engine trainer. The model was flyable and used a windup elastic band to power the propeller. The balsa frame was covered with thin paper and overall looked quite real once I applied the decals and markings to the wings and fuselage.

Putting together that little model taught me a lot about aircraft design. I became familiar with the terminology of the various components it takes to make a plane: spars, ribs, ailerons, and elevators, to name a few. After countless hours of construction, I was ready for the first test flight. My friends and I chose the road in front of our house, devoid of traffic for the most part, as the runway. I wound up the propeller, putting a few extra turns into the rubber band to get maximum thrust and duration of flight. Then I positioned the airplane facing into the wind in the center of the road and released the propeller. The takeoff was smooth, and soon it was airborne! As it headed skyward, a gust of wind turned it toward our apple tree. Fortunately for both plane and tree, the propeller stopped and the plane glided to a crash landing on the lawn. Further flights required repair of the landing gear and, on a few occasions, the skin of the airplane. After one particularly catastrophic crash landing, I wrote off the airframe and decided to retire the plane altogether. The best conclusion was a commemorative fire.

Not discouraged by my first foray into flight, I wanted to progress to faster aircraft, which meant getting my parents to buy me a control line Cox engine-powered P-40 Kittyhawk, the RAF version of the Warhawk. Its Super Bee engine produced around 0.057 hp at 13,500 rpm and sounded like a swarm of a thousand bees. Starting the engine

My friends (left) and I (right) trying to start the P-40 Warhawk. We lost many similar aircraft in our bid to fly faster and higher.

involved turning the propeller against the resistance of the starting spring and releasing it in a manner that got your finger out of the way. It took a couple of prop-finger impacts to figure that out.

Despite my best efforts, I was never very good at flying that aircraft. The principle was clear: lines went from a hand controller to the port wing of the airplane into the fuselage and down to the elevators. The rudder was in a fixed position that would keep the aircraft turning in a counterclockwise circle once airborne. It was straightforward in theory, but no one mentioned how dizzy you'd get as you watched the plane spin around and around in a circle until the engine ran out of gas and it was time to land. I still associate every flight of that aircraft with dizziness that can only be rivaled by spinning around in circles like a dervish. My landings were never very elegant, either, and after more than a few crashes the P-40 had to be retired as well.

In the absence of more sophisticated flight control systems, I transitioned from aircraft to model cars. This transition was hastened the moment I laid eyes on a Jetex 50 solid-fuel rocket motor on display at Ted's Hobby Shop. I suspect you're thinking that a rocket motor is not what a ten-year-old should be playing with, but what the heck: this was the sixties, and there was no paranoia about toys and liability. It took a while to save up for the engine, but between my allowance—a hefty ten cents a week—and my paper route, I was able to save up and buy it.

A car is a great vehicle, but it just wasn't enough for me. I wanted to make a car that was more than a car. What about a car with rocket propulsion? A fantastic idea, or so I thought. I glued the base of the engine to one of my plastic model cars, then went back out to the test track/runway/road in front of our house and put the car down facing a hill. Surely climbing the long hill would prevent my monster machine from getting too out of control. I had no idea how long the solid rocket propellant would last. It probably said in the instructions, but I was too excited to read them in detail.

Unlike the launch of a space-bound rocket, during which there is a sequenced countdown, I opted to light a match, hold it to the back of the rocket, and watch what would happen. The rocket ignited with a puff of smoke and the car took off with acceleration that would rival the best dragsters of the day. The car went in a straight line for about five seconds, enough to head up the hill at an impressive speed. That's when disaster struck. My glued-on engine mount ignited, turning the entire back end of the plastic car into a fireball, which then changed course and veered toward our neighbor's hedge. The impact was memorable: I used my jacket to smother the flames of my now-molten car and sputtering rocket. When I went inside later, my mom asked how I got burn marks on my jacket. I kept my explanation characteristically vague.

After numerous failed launch attempts and more than a few finger burns, I retired the Jetex 50 engine to my pyre of technological nonstarters. But even now I don't think of these experiments as complete failures. I learned something from each attempt. I learned what to do and what not to do. I learned that I'd have to pay with real pocket money for each screwup I made. And I learned how to put out small fires fast before my mother caught sight of the flames. As it turns out, failures both large and small are much more instructive than success.

3

A Great Day to Be Alive

As astronauts, we jokingly say that if you have a problem in outer space, you have the rest of your life to solve it. Some hear that and feel panic; others, like me, shrug their shoulders and get to work. Neither response is better, by the way. But they are different. Astronauts tend to focus more on finding a solution to the problem at hand than on the possibility of death looming right around the corner. Maybe it's the training. We're taught to operate complex systems, recognize failures, and be ready to intervene in worst-case scenarios. We spend as much time in simulators training for what can go wrong as we do for when things go according to plan.

I'm often asked if I was scared during liftoff on space missions or when I was out of the shuttle on space walks, attached to the International Space Station by only a thin tether. There is no question that during launch, when you're sitting on top of a massive controlled explosion, the realization that you're going to blast off, then accelerate to twenty-five times the speed of sound—and that things could go *very wrong*—commands your attention. It is scary. It is a stark reminder that courage comes from doing things that are frightening.

"I could never do that," I'm often told. "I could never be an astronaut. It's too risky."

What can I say? It's true! But life is full of risks. And in the space program, we don't take unnecessary chances. We learn to manage risks, consciously seeking to identify and mitigate every one of them to the best of our ability.

So here are three important things I've learned about managing risks. The first is this: If you're going to go skydiving, it's better to tell your parents *after* you jump, not before. Second, if it's your time for something bad to happen, it's your time. And if it's not, it's not. And finally, if you're in a life raft trying to survive and someone hands you a life preserver, take it.

Let me explain. As part of our ongoing astronaut training, the Canadian Space Agency (CSA) sent us to survival camp in the woods by Cold Lake, Alberta, in the middle of winter. Cold Lake is an understatement. With the wind chill, it was minus 40 degrees and the trees were covered in mounds of snow. A group of Canadian astronauts—Mike McKay, Julie Payette, Bjarni Tryggvason, and I—were training with a group of Canadian Forces personnel. The course was designed to teach us how to survive if we had to bail out of an aircraft flying over Northern Canada in the winter. We had a parachute to make a lean-to with, a sleeping bag, a knife, matches, and the contents of an aircraft survival kit. We also had whatever we could remember from the instructors' lessons. We certainly had no food, so we had to figure out what we could catch or forage to eat. We had to boil ice and snow to drink. The goal was to stay alive in the woods for three days and not get hurt or die from hypothermia, thirst, or, worst of all, your own stupidity. I learned a lot from that experience—such as how close you can get to the warmth of a fire without actually setting yourself aflame. It's an important life skill, I'd say.

Later, during our NASA ASCAN (astronaut candidate) training, we did water survival in Pensacola, which sounded easy after surviving Cold Lake. All my classmates were taken off the coast of Florida in a U.S. Navy ship. Then we each took turns being sent up in a parachute while the ship was traveling into the wind at about 20 knots. I was a couple of hundred feet up when our instructor released the cord, the only thing holding me to the ship. As the ship sailed away, I floated down and landed in the water, isolated and alone. I could barely see the others spread out in the distance where they had floated down in the ocean. The first thing I had to do was inflate my raft. Astronauts are a little competitive, so all of us were trying to see who could inflate their raft the fastest. We knew the instructors would track our progress, and we wanted to be sure we performed well.

One of my colleagues set up his raft just fine and managed to float in the open waters for a couple of hours, maybe longer. He had only about two more hours to go. So there he was, floating along, when a sailboat spotted him. Of course, they saw he was in a survival raft, so they figured something had gone horribly wrong.

"Hey!" they yelled out. "We can help you! You're going to be okay. Let's get you on board."

"Oh, not to worry," he responded. "I'm actually fine. I'm doing my astronaut survival training. This is just practice."

"What? That's so incredible! That's absolutely amazing . . . Would you like a sandwich?"

He thought about it. When you haven't eaten for a while, and you've been floating around in the sea on your own in the heat and sun, the thought of a sandwich will make you salivate instantly. But he said, "No, I don't think I'm supposed to accept that."

And they said, "Well, would you like to come aboard for a beer?"

Beer. Cold, thirst-quenching beer. But he remained adamant. "No, no. I'm pretty sure that's against the rules."

After a few more offers of assistance, the boat gave up and sailed away, leaving him to bob along the surface, neither hydrated nor fed.

He made it through the rest of the exercise, returning to the base safe and sound. All of us were gathered there, having completed the training as well.

"So?" our instructors asked. "How did everything go?" We were invited to share stories about our experiences on the water. That's when we heard all about the sailboat incident. "And," my colleague announced proudly, "I declined their offers of sandwiches. And beer."

"You did what?" one instructor said.

"I turned down their help. And their offer of food and the drink. I said I didn't want to come aboard."

The instructor shook his head. "Okay," he said. Then he paused.

"What?" my colleague asked. "What did I do wrong?"

"Here's an important tip," the instructor said. "If you're in a life raft in a survival situation and a boat comes up to you and offers help, you should take the help."

We all laughed then, which is easy to do after you've made it through a test of survival. Here he was thinking he'd be cheating if he accepted a cold beer, a sandwich, and a cushy ride back to the dock in a sailboat. But the instructor was right: when your life's at stake, there's no such thing as cheating.

Being in harm's way gives you a different perspective on life. General Jefferson Davis Howell, who was the director of the Johnson Space Center for three years, understood this. He guided the center through the difficult days after the loss of *Columbia* on February 1, 2003. I'll never forget when he started meetings saying: "It's a great day to be alive." Once, I was giving a presentation to a health association and I started the lecture with General Howell's line. "It's a great day to be alive in Toronto!" I said, looking around at the sea of confused faces. *What's so great about it?* they were thinking.

"When you've been in harm's way," I explained, "and you're still alive, *every* day is a good day."

I truly believe that, and I try to live by that credo. For many who have survived major illnesses or injuries, gratitude for the time you have left becomes a practice. Your standard for what a good day is changes. For me, instead of focusing on all the things I don't have or haven't achieved, I try to focus on what I *do* have and *have* done. For me, every day that I'm healthy and alive and able to contribute is a great day.

Throughout most of my childhood, I got by on luck. My friends and I had perhaps a different understanding of the rules of safety and risk management. It wasn't uncommon for us to hike along the railway tracks or put pennies on the rails to see how flat the penny would get. But our adventures seldom resulted in serious injury. That changed for me in grade five. One morning I rode to school on my bike, my mother's daily plea of "Be careful" ringing behind me, my book bag swinging back and forth on my back. I made it all the way to school, but as I approached the parking lot—*wham!* A car slammed into me, throwing me off my bike and knocking me down on the street. It was as though the car had come out of nowhere. I later learned that the driver had turned onto the road I was on and accelerated quickly.

I knew I was in trouble as soon as I found myself on the ground. I was shaken and had abrasions all over my arms and legs. The strap of my book bag was torn and my bike was bent into a strange shape. I was crying so hard that the bystanders must have thought I was badly hurt. But really I was crying because I knew in my heart that I had messed up, and I was mad at myself.

Perhaps I hadn't been careful enough when I looked both ways before I got hit, but it definitely took on a new meaning for me after that. Years later, when I was working at NASA, I was flying a twin-engine airplane back to William P. Hobby Airport in Houston. I landed safely and was ready to taxi back to the hangar to park. To get there, though, I had to cross two active runways.

"Hobby ground, Baron 92T on taxiway Juliet requesting permission to taxi back to the west ramp," I radioed to the ground controller.

"You're cleared to backtrack on 04," came the reply. "Taxi via Hotel 2, left on Hotel, cleared across runway 35, and taxi to the ramp. Have a great day."

Good. I was approved to head all the way back and park the aircraft. I taxied across the first runway and followed the controller's instructions to arrive at the second one. When I got there, just to be safe, I called ground again to double-check. They confirmed: "Cleared across runway 35 and taxi to the ramp. Have a great day."

I looked at the approach end of the runway and didn't see any planes coming. But as I taxied across, I started to hear the roar of a jet. That's when I looked over my shoulder and saw a 737 hurtling toward me from the opposite end of the runway. I moved my plane off the runway quickly and the other aircraft roared by. I could feel the ground shaking as it passed.

I parked my plane in a safe spot and got out. One of the ground crew was staring at me, wide-eyed.

"Did you see that 737?" he asked.

"I sure did. I was cleared to cross, so I'm not sure why he was taking off," I said, shaking a little.

"That was pretty close."

I was sure glad that I'd looked both ways before crossing that street. Childhood lessons do pay off.

It made me think back to another formative brush with death that I'd had at the early age of fifteen. It was 1969, the year thousands of young Americans—literally teens who were not of legal drinking age—were sent to Vietnam and found themselves in combat, never to make it home again. But the futility of that war was not as clear then as it is now. At home, my mother talked about the Second World War. It was a war she had lived through, one that had affected both her and my father profoundly. My parents believed there are times when we have a moral duty to fight, and they certainly viewed the Second World War as one of those times. My father's stepbrother had fought in the war. He was an able-bodied seaman who was killed aboard the HMCS *Margaree* after the ship collided with a freighter while trying to avoid U-boats. Neither of my parents ever forgot that.

As a teen, I joined the Royal Canadian Army Cadets out of a sense of duty that was instilled in me at home. I was part of the Royal Montreal Regiment and that summer was sent to the Canadian Forces base at Valcartier, Québec, for a couple of months of training. I remember the pride I felt when I donned my very first uniform. It was made of wool similar to those that had been used in the Second World War—actually, in all probability it might have been surplus from twenty years earlier. It was warm, itchy, and heavier than cotton fatigues, but I felt privileged to wear it. I felt like I was part of something bigger, joining the ranks of Canadians who had fought valiantly for their country.

On one of our training excursions in Valcartier, about a dozen of us kids were in the back of a "deuce and a half," an M35 cargo truck that was used for troop transport, similar to the ones that you see on the TV show *M*A*S*H*. We'd completed a twenty-five-mile

Every time I pulled on my Army Cadets uniform, I felt a swell of pride as I remembered the history and sacrifice of those who had come before me.

forced march that day. It was a nice day out, a few clouds but mostly sunny. Before we left that morning, we were ordered to take ponchos. *What do we need to take ponchos for?* we wondered with the wisdom of fourteen-year-old weather forecasters. I did as I was told, but I also made sure to take my first aid kit. My mother's lessons went deep, and there was no way I was going to be out on a march without my first aid kit in my bag.

We drove quickly through the woods back to the base, the green canvas covers on the trucks flapping in the wind. As we approached one of the sharper S-curves on the road, the truck started to fishtail. The wheels on the left side hit the soft shoulder and the vehicle rolled over. I was seated toward the back, facing the right side of the vehicle, and as the truck rolled I leaned forward and grabbed the front of the seat beneath me. I curled into a little ball and tried to hold myself in place. It didn't work, and after the equivalent of a backward somersault, I found myself thrown from the vehicle, stunned, in long grass about ten feet away from the now overturned truck, my bag still over my shoulder.

There was an eerie silence punctuated by the hissing and creaking of hot metal. I could taste blood in my mouth and felt it pooling on the shoulder of my uniform. My ears were ringing. Where was I? Once the worst of the shock passed, I willed myself to move. I had trouble raising my right arm, but my limbs all worked. I pushed myself up and was surprised to find I could walk. It was strangely dark. The swirling dust was so thick that it had blotted out the sun.

I walked around our overturned vehicle—two and a half tons of twisted, wrecked metal. A few officers were doing the same. I could hear cries all around me.

One officer yelled, "Does anybody have a first aid kit?"

"Yeah, I do!" I said, coming back to my senses and fishing through my bag for it. There were all these kids around—some of them obviously injured and others seemingly fine. I brought the first aid kit to the lieutenant, and the contents were rapidly used on me and a number of my colleagues.

We were loaded onto another troop transport and taken to the base hospital for assessment. By that time I was having difficulty lifting my right arm above my shoulder and a large bump had formed on the back of my head. I was X-rayed and my cuts and scrapes cleaned and bandaged. The next day I felt aches and pains, but that's it. This was my second close brush with death at an early age. I had lost my childhood sense of immortality, but fortunately nothing more.

In May 1968, two days after my fourteenth birthday, I went diving off the coast of Maine with a buddy of mine, Bryan Todd, the only other kid I knew who got his diving license so young. We were diving in the cold, steely-blue springtime water with a group from the YMCA. We were about thirty or forty feet down, exploring the sandy bottom for lobsters, when we found a mask on the ocean floor. Bryan and I looked at each other: this was kind of weird.

We surfaced as quickly as we could, and as soon as we reached the top, we noticed a commotion on the beach. A relatively inexperienced diver in his early fifties, from a different group diving in the same area, had been found unconscious in the surf. There were people surrounding him, attempting resuscitation. The coast guard arrived, but unfortunately it was too late. Despite everyone's best efforts, he died. We never knew the cause of death for sure, but he may have had a heart attack while trying to get back to shore. He was not wearing a buoyancy compensator and likely got into distress after surfacing.

This hit me, Bryan, and the rest of our group hard, of course. My father quietly spoke to Bryan and me after the event. "Despite what happened today, it's important to remember why you started diving and your love of exploring. Tomorrow you're scheduled for another dive, and I think you both should go."

I considered my dad's words carefully, and I felt he was right. We met with our whole diving group to discuss whether we would continue our trip as planned. Everyone agreed we should continue. Later that evening my father wrote an addendum in my logbook. "NEVER dive without an inflatable vest," he wrote. "One experienced diver must always accompany each novice in open water. No novice should be allowed to go too far out or below thirty feet until they are experienced and knowledgeable."

This was my dad's way of dealing with death at a close range—by making sure I learned something from it and would be better prepared for my next dive.

Part of an explorer's belief is to keep moving forward when things don't go well, to learn from an experience and move on. Rather than make me fear death, these early-life experiences made me philosophical. You never really know when your time will come, so why worry? As an astronaut, there have been times when I've wondered, *Is it my time?* I'm glad to report that today is another great day to be alive, and I hope tomorrow will be, too.

4

Failure Is the Best Teacher

In space, mistakes can be deadly. Outer space is an environment that does not tolerate error. A single mistake on a space walk or a miscalculation during a flight can be catastrophic. Astronauts train extensively before missions to ensure we know how to respond if things go wrong. But as I mentioned earlier, failure can be instructive. As we prepare for spaceflight, we use simulators to train like we fly so that, ultimately, we fly like we train. In the simulators, we learn from our mistakes so we can prevent errors in space. If you're willing to open yourself up to it, to accept feedback and reflect on your errors, you can learn so much.

I graduated from high school in 1971. The decade had started with turmoil. The Vietnam War dragged on, the Apollo missions were coming to an end, Nixon was in power in the U.S., and the drug scene was booming. I mostly avoided trouble; I was what you might call a "good kid." My marks were fine, I was working as a lifeguard and lifesaving instructor, and I had just started at McGill University. I always tried to toe the line and do the right thing. Still, I felt lost and restless.

I had applied to Carleton University in Ottawa, but that August, just before I was about to start school, my dad got sick. We were living in Montréal at the time, and it didn't seem right to be far away. I wanted to be close to home in case my family needed me.

"I'm withdrawing from Carleton," I announced to my parents. "I want to switch to a university closer to home."

"What do you mean? You were really excited about going to Carleton," they said.

"I'll be fine." I didn't want my dad to know that I was worried about his health and that I thought it would be better if I stayed nearby.

"First the long hair, then the motorcycle. Now this. You need some direction for your life." I rolled my eyes and thought about how much longer the conversation was going to last.

The same conversation had played out between my dad and me several times already and would continue until he passed away at an early age in 1976. He wanted me to smarten up and commit to something. I wanted to throw on my leather jacket and ride my motorcycle to the airport, where I'd started flying lessons at Laurentide Aviation. Every day we seemed to grow a little farther apart. I was young and was still so naïve. I had no idea then that my father was looking out for me.

Despite my attitude, I did see some wisdom in my dad's words. I switched to McGill and when I started, began to envision a career in life sciences or medicine. It would combine my love of physiology with an opportunity to save lives. I remember the excitement I felt going to

In 1972, I was young and carefree. All I wanted to do was throw on
my helmet, ride my motorcycle, and learn how to fly.

my first class, Biology 101. The class size was so large that it was held
in the Leacock Amphitheatre, the largest classroom on campus. I sat
in the back of the room looking down at the distant professor over an
ocean of heads. "Welcome to Biology 101. How many of you want to
be doctors?" he asked.

A waving sea of arms resulted, almost the entire room of students.
How could I ever succeed when everyone else wanted to do what I
was hoping to do? The long-ago anatomy lessons of my childhood and
learning the physiology of diving did not make me feel any more confident. I felt lost. How would I overcome the odds when university alone
was hard enough?

The first couple of years at McGill were very difficult. I was working part-time twice a week at Pointe-Claire Aquatic Centre to earn enough money to pay my tuition. I had to stop flight training for my private pilot's license because I couldn't afford it. It was either become a pilot or stay at McGill and maybe one day become a doctor. I never thought I'd be able to do both. As for flying in space, well, that had become a boyhood fantasy that didn't stand a chance against the realities of life.

"What are you doing?" my dad asked one morning, looking at the closed book on the couch beside me.

"Studying," I replied as I gazed out the window.

Everything seemed to be falling apart. I was balancing two part-time jobs to pay for my tuition while trying to study. When my marks came in at the end of the year, I was barely passing. If they didn't improve, I would never be accepted to medical school, and if they got worse, I risked getting kicked out of the university. I needed to get

As much as I hated having to give up my pilot lessons, I knew it had to happen if I was going to one day become a doctor. I still dreamed of returning to the cockpit and, someday, maybe even flying to space.

better at managing my time and studying effectively. I was determined to prove myself.

I moved to an apartment in downtown Montréal. It was on Drummond Street—well, sort of on Drummond street. To get to it, you had to turn right in the first alley off Drummond, just north of Sherbrooke Street, then take a left in the next alley and go halfway down to find yet another very small alley that led to a door. Sixty dollars a month got me one room with a tiny kitchenette in the corner and a small bathroom in the other. I was still hoping to be a doctor but I knew one thing for sure: I didn't want to be a failure.

It wasn't easy. By that point my dad and I had drifted so far apart that he'd effectively cut me off. He was retired, and my mom was supporting the family financially. She helped me out when she could, but mostly I was on my own, and money was tight. Each night I would drive my motorcycle home from the library and park it in the alley outside my front door. In the winter I'd walk. I'd make a pot of macaroni and cheese and crack open my books again to study late into the night. In my lowest moments, after I turned off the lights, I would lie in bed, stare at the ceiling feeling completely alone, and think, *So this is my life...*

During Christmas of my last year of undergrad, I went home to see my family. I was no longer living downtown, having moved to a suburb on the West Island by Macdonald College, where I was doing an undergraduate research project at McGill's Institute of Parasitology. The excitement of having my own research project made up for the long trip to the main McGill campus downtown, but commuting stretched my already thin budget.

I had a full turkey dinner with my family and we spent the evening catching up. The atmosphere was strained. When it was time for me to head back to my place, my mom called me into the kitchen.

"Take this with you," she said, handing me a paper bag with leftovers in it.

"Keep the leftovers for you and Dad. I'll be fine."

"Just take them. I know you could use them."

I trudged down the street toward the highway, the bag clenched in my fist. I didn't have enough money for bus or taxi fare home, but I didn't tell my parents. Instead, I huddled at the edge of the road and stuck out my thumb. I'd been hitchhiking a lot that winter. My motorcycle worked well in the summer, but it wasn't all that helpful in the depths of a Montréal snowstorm.

I stood in one spot, hoping for a pair of headlights to slow down. The entire landscape was barren. Suddenly I realized that this could be the rest of my life. *Is this as good as it gets? Do you want to live on the roadside, Dave?* I thought. *Or do you want to do something about it?* I wasn't owed anything by anyone. It was clearly up to me to figure things out. So I did.

By the end of senior year of my undergraduate degree, my grades were good enough to earn me a spot as a graduate student in the department of physiology at McGill working with Dr. Bernardo Dubrovsky, a neurophysiologist and physician. While many researchers become super-specialists, Bernardo was the antithesis—an unconventional researcher with a wide range of interests in clinical and fundamental neuroscience. My first year of the program was nirvana. By day I was studying neuroscience, and by night I was drinking sangria with my fellow graduate students. Life was rosy.

One day Bernardo came into the lab to ask me if I'd be interested in applying to a NASA request for research proposals to study attentiveness in pilots and astronauts. It sounded like a good plan to me. We submitted the proposal, and I began my first NASA research project. My boyhood dream sparked back to life.

That first year went by quickly. But while I was enjoying my research, not everything was going well. My father's health had deteriorated. Our relationship continued to have its ups and downs, but one day that spring, a few months before he died, he called unexpectedly.

"Would you like to get together sometime in the next couple of weeks?" he asked. "Perhaps I could come into town. We could have lunch and maybe do a little shopping." He sounded tentative. I wasn't sure how to react.

"Sure, that'd be great," I said. My dad had become more supportive the closer I got to graduation, and we were starting to enjoy our time together again. That day was fantastic. We had lunch at Moishes steakhouse, went shopping up and down Sainte-Catherine Street, and finished off with a beer in a brasserie. We never once talked about the future. Maybe Dad knew he didn't have much time. Maybe he wanted one more great day together. Whatever his plan, that was the most memorable day of my life spent with my father.

It was also one of the last. Six months later, in September 1976, he passed away. My mother, sister, and I all grieved for him our own ways.

It was the beginning of a difficult period. My mother had two car accidents in the first three months after my dad's death. Every time the phone rang, I was worried something else had happened. A year later I was still healing. At the same time I was also preparing to take a major test at school, one that would allow me to go directly into a PhD program. I worked through countless study sessions, determined to succeed and make my dad proud of me.

Exam day arrived and I found myself in front of the committee. I started my presentation with excitement, enthusiastic to share the results of my research, but as the presentation went on, I began to get the feeling it wasn't going well. The adjudicators seemed unimpressed with my work, and their questions got increasingly critical.

"Thank you very much. I don't believe we have any further questions," the head adjudicator said curtly when I finished. "We will discuss your presentation and let you know our decision later today."

I left the room with a growing sense of despair. Later in the day, I received the news: I had failed the presentation. I would not go on to pursue a PhD.

I was devastated, and not just because I'd failed the exam. Shortly after, my application to medical school was rejected. When you fail an exam to get into a PhD program, it doesn't look good on your résumé.

I spent the next few weeks thinking to myself, *This is it. You're stuck at the side of the road forever.* This dark thought was then followed by *Maybe Dad was right. Maybe I don't have what it takes.* Eventually, though, my self-pity turned to something else: anger. If the committee wasn't going to allow me to pursue a PhD, fine. I would take that anger and use it to propel me to greater things. I would prove to them that I could excel in physiology.

One Saturday night I was studying in the library when a girl put her books down at my table. I risked a glance at her, and we smiled sheepishly at each other.

"I didn't think anyone else studied on a Saturday night," I said.

"I like the quiet," she said.

"I'll leave you to it, then."

"What are you working on?" she asked, leaning closer.

"Just studying for an exam in physiology."

"Want a study partner?"

We talked the rest of the night, and as we left the library I asked for her number. We saw each other a few more times, and then, a few weeks later, we were at dinner, when the conversation I'd been hoping to avoid came up.

"Dave, I think we should get serious in this relationship," she said.

I thought about what that future would look like. There would be fun moments: talking about movies over a glass of wine or wandering the city's parks on a weekend. But deep down I knew I wanted something more. Unfortunately, I wasn't all that great at articulating my emotions.

"I'm sorry," I said. "I want to, but I can't."

"What do you mean you can't?"

"I need to focus on finishing my degree. It's hard to explain, but it means everything to me right now. I can't let anything or anyone take me away from that. I'm sorry."

The rest of the night was a bit of a train wreck. But as difficult as the conversation was, I knew it was the right decision.

I had one final exam left to prove myself. All the students in the program—master's and PhD alike—had to take the same test, a comprehensive written examination in physiology. Some felt it was a daunting task, as it required a deep knowledge of all areas of physiology, not just one area of research expertise.

I'm going to beat every single one of them, I promised myself. I blocked everything else out of my life. I devoted all of my energy to my studies, reading and making notes on every physiology textbook I had.

I wrote the final exam a couple of months later, and when the results were posted, I scanned the list for my student ID number. Knowing the scores were ranked from best to worst, I ran my finger along the paper starting from the bottom. But I couldn't find my student number. *Where am I? Did I fail again?* I wondered as my finger traced higher. I was about to start panicking, but then I reached the top of the list . . . and there I was. I'd done it—I'd proven to myself that I could persevere and earned the top mark on the exam! I laughed with a mixture of joy and relief. All of that work and sacrifice had been worth it.

As I walked home, I felt lighter than I had in months. I was back on the road, not in the ditch. And the exam wasn't an end—perhaps it was a beginning. I had felt what it was like to fail, and I had seen the power of resilience and commitment. I wondered what might happen if I continued to carry that same grit and determination with me when facing other challenges. What else might I be able to do?

I still saw medicine as a fantastic opportunity. *Maybe things will be different now,* I thought. I had the top mark of all the graduate students in the physiology department. That must count for something.

I decided to apply to medical school again. I wrote a heartfelt letter to accompany my application, secured support from a number of my professors, and then held my breath. As the winter turned to spring, I received letters of acceptance from both McGill and Queen's University. My persistence had paid off, and I wrote back to McGill accepting their offer to start medical school in September 1979.

Suddenly my life had new direction and purpose, both professionally and personally. The year before, I had met Cathy. We'd met at the Pointe-Claire pool, but when I'd finished working there in December 1978, I figured that was it and we'd never see each other again. Then, in January, I had heard from her and decided to ask her out on a date. I was really excited when I picked her up in my car, which I'd purchased for $50 and painted using spray cans from Canadian Tire.

Cathy hopped in and said, "Impressive car. What's the deal with the sock?"

The driver's side door didn't close and I couldn't afford to fix it, so I'd tied a sock around the handle and kept the other end tucked under my leg to stop the door from flying open while I drove.

"A few mechanical issues I haven't had a chance to fix yet."

We made it into downtown Montréal without any incident, where we had souvlaki and bagels. We dated regularly after that, and while I was crazy about Cathy, I was also worried about our relationship. I had a burning drive to succeed and make something of myself. What kind of a woman would want to be with some guy who spent his life in the library?

"Cathy, I care about you," I said as things between us progressed. "Which is why I want to be honest. I've always wanted to go to medical school. And when I do, I'm going to have to give it everything I have. I might not be around a lot. There will be times when it will seem like I'm living in the library." That was it, I figured. It would now be over.

"That doesn't bother me at all," she replied.

My eyebrows jumped up. "It doesn't?"

Cathy grinned. "When I was in high school, I told my guidance counselor I wanted to be a pilot. Do you know what the counselor said?"

"'Go for it'?"

"Not quite. He said, 'You're a woman. You can be a flight attendant, or maybe an engineer, but you can't be a pilot.'"

I couldn't believe my ears. "That's ridiculous."

"Exactly. So I decided right then and there that I would become a pilot."

Wow. *Now, that is some woman,* I thought to myself. If anyone was going to understand me, it would be her. "So you get where I'm coming from?"

"Of course I do, Dave. We'll be fine. Nothing is going to stop us from following our dreams."

It had been a long, difficult road getting to where I was, and the future was filled with uncertainty. But I was starting to recognize that anything in life that's worth doing is hard. And the harder it is, the greater meaning it will bring. I had failed. I had experienced despair. But I finally knew what I wanted. Now, a bit like Cathy, I just had to go make it happen. With a woman like Cathy by my side, as driven and focused on her own path as I was on mine, I felt better. I knew we could get through anything together.

PART TWO

5

The Astronaut Killer

So much of being an astronaut is about what's next: the next step in a checklist, the next test, the next mission . . . Astronauts and doctors are trained to block out any worry about what might come in the future and look only at what's happening right now. Focus is critical. On a mission, that approach keeps us alive and helps us operate in an environment where a single distraction or disruption can be deadly. It's also a mind-set I've learned as an emergency physician and use in my day-to-day life. Wherever I find myself, I try to be fully present in the moment and see each challenge as a new opportunity.

It's that sort of thinking that started me on the path to becoming an astronaut in the first place. I graduated from medical school in 1983 and the same year finally received my master's degree in physiology. I learned that it's what you do when you don't succeed that determines whether you will one day succeed. At graduation I won the Wood Gold Medal as the top clinical student and the psychiatry prize. I was now a university scholar, and the physiology department had put me on the dean's honor list for my master's degree. There had been some discussion about having me submit a thesis for a PhD, but after my previous failed oral presentation, I didn't want to go through a PhD defense. It was time to move on. I was thrilled to be a physician and ready for the next stages of my clinical training.

Cathy and I moved to Ottawa—our first time living together—so that I could start my residency in family practice and emergency medicine while she finished her pilot instructor's rating and taught flying lessons. She had her commercial pilot's license, and there was no better way to build the hours she needed to become an airline pilot than through teaching others how to fly.

My family practice residency went by in a blur of rotations and postings in various departments. Some of them, like emergency medicine, anesthesia, and critical care medicine, I considered potential career paths. Others showed me what I didn't want to do.

Cathy and I married in May 1986 and I became a fully licensed doctor a couple of months later. That July, I started another residency with the Royal College of Physicians and Surgeons of Canada,

Cathy and I winter camping in 1985.

specializing in emergency medicine at the University of Toronto. Cathy started working as a flight instructor at Buttonville Municipal Airport in Markham, Ontario, and continued building hours and experience to get a job flying with Air Canada in 1988. She was one of only a handful of women pilots with the company. She loved her job. I admired her skill as a pilot and was immensely proud of her for achieving her goal. She was also a member of the Ninety-Nines, the international organization of women pilots, and in 1991 the two of us went to the Women in Aviation International conference in Florida. The event was a chance for Cathy to spend time among her peers and mentors. I was happy to tag along as a proud "49½er" to have a chance to experience a part of her world.

One of the speakers at the conference was Linda Godwin, an American astronaut who had flown in space just a few months earlier. Linda is a renowned physicist—and, like Cathy, a member of the Ninety-Nines. During Linda's mission, she and the rest of the crew ran into some unexpected equipment malfunctions. They solved everything and ultimately had a very successful mission. My steps got faster and faster the closer Cathy and I got to the auditorium, and when Linda started speaking, it brought me back to my unfulfilled childhood dream.

Linda's speech was wrapping up when Cathy turned to me and said, "Why don't we try to talk to her?"

Without any hesitation I said, "I'd love to!"

What a fantastic opportunity! How many times in your life do you get a chance to speak to an astronaut who has just spent a week in space and orbited the earth ninety-three times? I decided to make the most of the moment. I took a spot in the line.

"Hello, I'm Dave Williams," I said when I finally reached Linda and shook her hand. I was excited to meet such an amazing woman and was interested to learn how she went from being a physicist to joining the space program.

"I'm an emergency physician," I said, "but I've been interested in becoming an astronaut for a long time."

"That's wonderful!" said Linda, nodding encouragingly. "And you're from Canada? Good news—from what I understand, the Canadian Space Agency is going to be recruiting a new group of astronauts next year."

I barely remember the rest of our conversation. Without knowing it, Linda had handed me an incredible opportunity.

"Maybe I'll apply!" I said to Cathy later.

Cathy laughed. "Yes, you should."

As soon I got back home, I called the Canadian Space Agency.

"I understand you're going to be hiring Canadian astronauts shortly. Where should I submit my résumé?"

"Thank you for your interest," said the manager at the CSA. "But we are not hiring any astronauts right now."

I felt disappointment right in my gut. Maybe Linda had false information?

"Dave, send the agency your résumé anyway," Cathy said.

She was right. What was the worst that could happen? They'd simply send me a rejection letter saying what I'd already heard on the phone. I took Cathy's advice and sent in a letter of interest and my résumé.

Months went by and I didn't hear anything. *So much for that,* I thought. Then, in January 1992, I was reading the *Globe and Mail* and saw a half-page ad: "The Canadian Space Agency Seeks Astronauts" read the headline. Linda had been right after all! Even though I had already applied, I didn't want to risk not following the process outlined in the ad, so I sent another letter and an updated copy of my résumé.

The selection process for astronauts is a long one. Months can go by between stages, and you can drive yourself crazy obsessing over what's next or what people are thinking about you. I decided that the best thing I could do while waiting was to enjoy the ride. It helped that I had a fantastic career and plenty to keep me busy. I'd recently become the director of the emergency department at Sunnybrook Hospital, and I loved the work. I felt I needed to talk with Tom Closson, the hospital's CEO, just to let him know what I was up to.

"Tom," I said. "I've applied to be an astronaut."

Tom looked at me. His eyebrows rose into an arch, which made him look surprised, although he's the kind of man who's rarely surprised by anything. But this time I think I had genuinely caught him off guard.

One second . . . five seconds . . . ten . . . then: "Are you kidding me, Dave? Is this a joke?" Tom saw me as a dedicated doctor, which I was.

"It's no joke, Tom," I said. When he realized I was serious, he shook his head and sighed.

"Okay, tell me more."

"Well, believe it or not," I began, "ever since I watched Alan Shepard lift off into space when I was a kid, I've dreamed of becoming an astronaut. And the Canadian Space Agency is recruiting, so . . . so I submitted my résumé."

Tom crossed his arms. A look of total skepticism filled his face. "What do you think your chances are?"

"There are around 5,300 applicants."

"In that case, I don't have to worry. I don't think I'm about to lose you. Just keep me in the loop. And good luck to you." Tom's "good luck" sounded highly cautionary. It sounded more like "Dave, don't get your hopes up."

But as the months went by, I dutifully kept Tom updated with whatever news I received. When I made it to the third phase alongside 370 other candidates, I passed the news on to Tom.

"Huh," he said, those eyebrows of his arching up even farther. "Keep me in the loop."

One hundred.

"Keep me in the loop."

Fifty.

"Really? You've made the fifty cut?"

Cathy, meanwhile, seemed not at all surprised that I was still among the shrinking candidate pool.

"Dave! That's fantastic! What happens now?" she asked.

"The agency is going to hold a meet-and-greet and panel interview for the applicants."

"Sounds like fun."

"It should be, but I'm curious about who the other candidates are. I'll bet they're all really qualified."

"Don't worry about them. You can only be yourself. And enjoy the event."

When I got to the event, I was surprised by the sheer number of reporters gathered in the lobby. There was widespread interest in the recruitment program, and it looked like every media outlet in the country had come out. I managed to slip past the cameras with a couple of quick interviews, the buzz from the reporters' voices and the hum of the cameras dimming as I closed the door behind me.

As I entered the main room, I saw the Canadian Space Agency logo displayed on the wall behind the microphone stand, and it reminded me of my dream of one day looking down at the earth from among the stars. I took a seat at one of the chairs and introduced myself to the man sitting beside me.

"Hi, I'm Dave Williams."

"Nice to meet you."

"Pretty incredible how many reporters are outside, isn't it?" I said.

"It's packed out there."

"So what do you do?" I asked the man.

"I'm a test pilot. My background is in oceanography, but I've served in the air force for fifteen years now."

My stomach dropped. A test pilot *and* a scientist? If everyone there was that qualified, what chance did I have? I excused myself and wandered around the room, chatting with the other tremendously qualified candidates. There were military personnel in full uniform, a number of engineers, and a couple of academics. Everyone was so exceptionally talented, I had to wonder, *Should I really be here? Am I good enough?*

An official from the CSA began the briefing, so I took to my seat again.

"Thank you all for joining us today," the official began. "We'll keep things brief so you have more time for interviews with the media. You'll each be scheduled for an interview with a seven-person panel sometime during the next two weeks, and we'll also be contacting you to set up a flight medical. Please note that there will be a documentary crew present throughout this period. The crew may ask you questions about your experiences, so feel free to answer them openly."

If I'd had a camera pointed at me just then and had been asked what I felt, it would have been an easy, one-word answer: intimidated. I didn't have much time to dwell on my thoughts, though, because as soon as the briefing was over, we went straight into a press conference. The doors opened up and the media flooded in. The reporters had their microphones in our faces and were asking rapid-fire questions: "Why do you want to be an astronaut? What skills would you bring to the job?"

"I can field that," said one of the candidates, jumping up and angling himself in front of a camera. Another candidate's head whipped around as this one, too, sought an open microphone. Was this what was expected? Were we all supposed to elbow our way past each other for time in front of the camera? I'm just not that guy. I couldn't help but think of my mother. One thing that has always frustrated her is my reluctance to share my accomplishments or good news. I simply found it weird to call her up and say, "Hey, look at this great thing I did." I'd rather be out doing things than talking about things I've already done.

I answered a couple of questions. Then, when the reporters stopped coming my way, I quietly moved along. I was leaning against the wall off to the side when a man I didn't know came over.

"Wow, they're pretty competitive, aren't they?" he said, hands clasped behind his back.

"They sure are," I said.

I turned toward this man to get a good look. His age and his glasses made it clear he wasn't one of the other applicants.

"Are you one of the candidates?" he asked.

"I am. I'm Dave Williams."

"Nice to meet you. I'm Bruce." He gestured at the other candidates in front of the cameras. "You're not going to get in there?"

"No," I said. "I've already answered a couple of questions and I'm happy to answer more, but I'm more interested in getting to meet everyone here."

My new acquaintance then changed topics. "Hey, have you heard about the plans for a new Canadarm?" I could hear the excitement in his voice.

Of course I had heard of it! "I've been following the Canadarm development since its first flight on *Columbia*. Actually, a few months ago, Linda Godwin gave a great talk about how her crew used the arm to deploy a new observatory during their mission."

"There's a new one under construction, to give the Canadian Space Agency a role in future missions to help build the Space Station," Bruce said.

I couldn't believe I'd found someone who was as excited about the recent space program developments as I was. "I'm looking forward to seeing that arm in action," I said.

"You sure I'm not keeping you from all that?" he asked, nodding at nearby reporters.

"No, that's fine, thanks. If the press wants to talk with me, they'll find me."

A few weeks later I got a call from the Canadian Space Agency—I'd made the final round of twenty candidates. It turned out that the man I'd been talking to was Bruce Aikenhead, head of the Canadian astronaut office. Bruce had probably been there to observe how the candidates reacted to the competition and to the press. A number of candidates hadn't spared him a second glance. Perhaps he remembered our discussion. Once again, a chance conversation potentially provided me with the opportunity of a lifetime.

When I broke the news to Tom, I thought his eyebrows were going to leap right off his face.

"It sounds like I might have to hire a new director after all," he said.

Later that night, Cathy and I broke down my chances.

"Twenty applicants left, and they'll narrow it down to six," Cathy said. "So you have, what, a 30 percent chance? No problem." I looked up and caught her huge smile.

"Something like that," I said. The odds weren't exactly in my favor, but Cathy's confidence buoyed me as I headed into the final stages.

The final weeklong round of tests and interviews were far more extensive than the previous ones had been. For the first time all the candidates from across the country would be gathered together. We met in Ottawa where we all stayed at the Westin hotel. Every applicant in that group of twenty was impressive in his or her own way. There were robotics experts, geophysicists, pilots, and other physicians. The CSA could have hired any one of them, and they would have done an outstanding job representing Canada in space. I was proud to be part of the group.

When I arrived for our first meeting, everyone was friendly, but there was a competitive atmosphere underneath it all, which built as the week wore on. Our first briefing was at 6:00 p.m. on a Sunday. We met in a conference room where a lavish buffet dinner had been set out. The day had been a whirlwind; many of us had arrived from out of town earlier in the day. There had been little time to think, never mind eat, so the smell of the food made our mouths water. But when the introductory remarks started, everyone's attention turned away from the food and toward the front of the room.

"Thank you for joining us this week," said William MacDonald ("Mac") Evans, the vice president of operations at the Canadian Space

Agency, who was leading the initial briefing. "Congratulations on making it this far. You're all accomplished candidates, and we know that it is going to be a difficult selection process with so many qualified applicants. Initially we thought we needed six astronauts, but after a careful review of the flight opportunities, we've decided to select just four astronauts to join the program."

Four candidates? That meant that only one out of every five of us was going to become an astronaut. Everyone's chance of getting selected had just dropped. I fought to stay calm.

Silence engulfed the room. A hand sprung up. "With the Space Station program on the horizon, won't the CSA need *six* astronauts?" asked the candidate.

Mac shifted his weight. "We think it's important to have a realistic flight opportunity for each of the astronauts we hire. I recognize the announcement said there were six spots available, but in light of recent developments, we're able to select only four final candidates."

I watched the applicants around me do the same math in their heads as I had done. I saw the pilots in the group glancing at each other, trying to count how many people they'd be competing against, and the engineers did the same thing. We each had at least a 20 percent chance of securing a final spot, but the odds would be different depending on each person's background. They weren't going to pick four pilots and no engineers, or vice versa. I was about to start counting the medical professionals in the room and calculate my specific odds, but I stopped myself. *Dave, you've gotten this far in life by competing only against yourself, by always trying to do your best and not worrying about how others are doing. Just be the best version of yourself that you can be and maybe that will be enough. And if not, oh, well, you've got a great career as a physician.*

The briefing was winding down. It was now around 7:30 p.m.

"We're going to wrap up, but just one final point," said the CSA representative leading the talk. "At eight a.m. tomorrow, we'll begin your blood work for some of you. Those tests require fasting for twelve hours beforehand. See you tomorrow!"

With that, the briefing ended. So much for the buffet. Lucky for me, I didn't feel like eating. I went to bed that night with a rumbling stomach and a buzzing brain. But hunger couldn't dim my excitement.

The next day started with a battery of medical tests, then a press conference. After our blood work, a small group of us were led into a room where a doctor and a few assistants awaited.

"We're conducting a basic treadmill test," said the doctor. "We'll bring you in one at a time. Please follow the instructions and we'll have you out of here in no time."

I'm a doctor, so I knew the treadmill test was a straightforward evaluation of heart function. Still, I figured the others should know what they were getting into. Once the official doctor left, I turned to the group. "Just so you know, none of us are going to beat the treadmill."

I was greeted by a series of strange looks.

"What I mean is, this isn't a fitness test. We use this test all the time in the hospital. It's meant to screen for underlying heart disease and possible abnormal heart rhythms. Don't worry about trying to outdo the machine. Once you get to the target, it's better to get off as quickly as possible. If you stay on longer, something might turn up on the electrocardiogram, and you don't want that."

Some in the group seemed skeptical. They probably thought I was trying to mislead them or set them up to fail. One candidate tried to beat the treadmill and finally had to be assisted off after sprinting up a full incline to no avail. The treadmill always won. In subsequent astronaut selections the CSA added fitness testing to the process, but in 1992 the treadmill was a clinical test not a fitness test.

I completed the treadmill test, and it was time to get ready for the press conference. It was held in one of the large conference rooms at the hotel, and that was when I started to feel the competitive pressure.

The media approached the candidates they thought were most likely to succeed. One came over to me and asked, "Which one are you?"

"I'm Dave Williams, the emergency physician." I said.

"Oh, you're not the one I'm looking for," the reporter said, turning away to search for someone else.

It certainly made me wonder where I stood in the group.

Over the course of the next few days, all of us underwent trials in other areas as well. We did presentations to the panel on various topics. I gave mine half in English and half in French, as I thought it was important to demonstrate proficiency with both official languages. Psych evaluations—all smooth there. I was bonding with the other candidates, and while I didn't know where I stood in the eyes of the selection committee, by my own standards I was happy with how I was doing.

On Wednesday morning I was scheduled for the most important medical test for astronauts: the eye exam. The test is known as "the Astronaut Killer" because of how many candidates are ruled medically inadmissible after failing the eye test. Needless to say, none of us looked forward to our turn in the ophthalmologist's chair.

I leaned against the wall as I waited in the examination room for the eye doctor. I was feeling somewhat confident, as I knew my eyesight was 20/20 and I'd already passed an aviation medical for my pilot's license. I was still getting used to my role as the patient, not the doctor, and fighting the desire to take over. I knew that a single finding from this test could wipe away all the good that had come before it.

"Good afternoon, Dave," said the doctor when he finally entered. "How are you feeling?"

"I'm great, thanks." *Positive thinking,* I told myself.

"Excellent. Let's get started, shall we?" He gestured at the slit lamp and took a seat across from me. "Would you mind putting your chin on the strap and looking into the machine?"

"How long have you been working with the Canadian Forces?" I asked, blinking hard as he turned on the light. All the medical tests

were conducted by CF physicians under the leadership of Dr. Gary
Gray, a military flight surgeon.

"I haven't been working here that long. In fact—and you might
not remember this—I was a resident at Sunnybrook while you were an
emergency physician there. You referred a few patients to me when I
was covering the emergency department."

"Really? What a small world!" I immediately felt more at ease.

"It'll look even smaller if you get to see it from space!" he said. "I
gather you're still at Sunnybrook?"

"I am."

"That was such a great place to train. I remember—"

The doctor abruptly stopped talking. When a doctor stops talking
in the middle of an examination, it's generally not a good sign.

"What did you find?" I asked.

"Nothing," he said.

"Oh, come on, I'm a doctor. I know how this works."

He sighed. "I can't say anything conclusively. But . . . there's no
easy way to tell you this . . . it looks like you might have benign paving
stone degeneration." As a physician, I knew immediately that he was
talking about a degenerative condition of the retina found in the pe-
riphery of the eye. It was listed as a "degenerative retinopathy" on the
list of disqualifying medical conditions.

I sat back in the chair and stared at the ceiling in silence. I recognized that the condition itself wasn't serious. But if the doctor was
right: I would likely be disqualified from the selection.

The doctor sensed my disappointment. "Nothing is for sure yet and
there are only a few small areas of the eye that are affected. I'm going
to send you to a retinal specialist, one of the best in Canada. We'll see
what he says."

I appreciated the doctor's optimism, but as I left the examination
room, my mind was clouded. I was so close to my goal! To find out
my own body might betray me was difficult news to digest. While he

arranged a visit to the specialist, I carried on with my remaining interviews, albeit with a new sobering clarity. It hit home that I had to savor every moment of this experience, because it was probably about to end. This was it: chances were I was never going to be an astronaut. *It's okay, Dave,* I told myself. *You're fortunate enough to have a great job, hobbies you enjoy, and a loving family.* I had such a great life, so I vowed not to be too sad if I was disqualified from the astronaut program. Life *would* go on, and it would *still* be great; for now, the possibility of becoming an astronaut seemed remote.

Later that week I received a call from Dr. Gray. The retinal specialist had spoken with his NASA counterpart. "Given that your case of degeneration is so mild, it might not be disqualifying," the specialist said. "We'll have a medical review board evaluate the high-resolution retinal photographs and make a decision by the end of the week. Perhaps it will work out for you."

I thanked him for the update. There was hope once again: hope that my eye condition would not disqualify me, hope that I might actually be good enough to be selected. Now I knew firsthand what it felt like to be a patient and to receive difficult news from a doctor. It would not be the last time or the worst health news I would receive from a doctor. For now, I put my emotions aside—all except hope—and kept working toward my goal.

The week passed by in a blur of morning runs by the Rideau Canal, presentations, and meetings with officials and astronauts from the CSA. Shortly before I left to go home, I learned that my eye issue had been officially cleared, which was a huge relief. But I had no idea how the rest of my interviews and tests had gone. All I knew was that I'd given it my best shot. I'd done everything in my power to present the best version of myself possible.

Life went back to normal. I returned to work, and two weeks later I was teaching an advanced cardiac life support course to a room full of nurses and doctors at Sunnybrook when my pager went off—pretty common for a doctor. I excused myself and went to one of the phones outside the lecture theater to call the hospital operator.

"You have an outside call," the operator said. "Remain on the line and I'll connect you."

It was 12:40. I'd been informed that the CSA would start calling candidates at noon. But was this the CSA or was it Cathy, or my mother, or a colleague? I would soon find out.

The call was connected. "Dave, it's Arline Marchand from the CSA. Do you have a moment to chat?" asked the voice on the other end of the line.

Are you kidding? There was no call more important to me at that moment! I tried to hide my excitement. "Of course," I said. "Happy to take a few minutes."

"We're pleased to let you know that you're one of the four candidates to be selected."

What? Really? I couldn't believe what I was hearing. It was incredible. "That's fantastic! I was worried that I wasn't selected, as I thought you'd call the successful candidates first," I said.

"I started to, but then I began to receive a number of calls from other candidates, so I'm a little delayed in calling you. Sorry."

"That's fine. I'm thrilled," I responded. "Thanks very much. It's an honor to be chosen."

I learned the names of the other candidates who'd been selected— Julie Payette, Chris Hadfield, and Rob Stewart. I was in a daze for the rest of the conversation.

"There's going to be a public announcement next week," the CSA representative said. "But until then, we'd ask that you don't share this news publicly."

"Can I let me wife know?"

"Yes, but don't tell anyone else. We don't want the news to get out before the official announcement."

"Of course," I said. "I'll look forward to hearing more details."

After the call, I took a moment to gather myself. I thought back to my childhood heroes, the pilots and astronauts who'd flown into space before me. I thought about the extraordinary things they had done and seen, and how I was one step closer to my dream of following in their footsteps.

Then I called Cathy to deliver the news. She picked up on the first ring.

"Dave, did you hear?"

"Yes, they called. I made it—I'm going to be an astronaut."

"Amazing! I'm so proud of you. Congratulations! There was never any doubt in my mind you'd be selected."

I'd had so many incredible things happen in my life, enjoyed so many great days, and overcome more than a few hurdles, but the news still seemed unbelievable.

"It's a great day," I said. "Let's celebrate later. I'll be home around five thirty." But in my head at that moment I was thinking about another day altogether, the day I was lucky enough to meet Cathy.

6

The Point of No Return

The official announcement about the four Canadians selected to be astronauts was scheduled for Monday, June 8, 1992, two days after I received the news. On Sunday morning I called my mother to let her know. Despite my reluctance to tell stories of my successes, this was something I had to share.

"Hi, Mom. How are things?" I asked.

"Fine. It's a beautiful day. I was just out having coffee on the deck." The year before, at age seventy, she'd moved to a stone farmhouse that sat on over twenty acres of land. "It's my little piece of Canada. I've always wanted to live in a stone farmhouse." She seemed to be really enjoying it.

"I have some news, Mom," I said. "I've been accepted by the Canadian Space Agency as one of the new astronauts."

There was a pause on the other end of the line. Even in the silence I could hear how pleased she was. "Congratulations," she said. "That's fantastic. Whenever you set your mind to doing something, you usually succeed." By now she was a veteran observer of my triumphs and failures.

"The announcement is tomorrow in Ottawa, so you can't tell anyone until then."

"Okay, I won't. Let me know if it's going to be on television. Love you and congratulations."

On that fateful Monday, Julie, Chris, Rob, and I all traveled to the capital for our debut performance as astronauts.

When I got to the meeting place, I was ushered into a side room where the four of us and a few other officials were gathering. I spied Chris's military crew cut from across the room and made my way over to the group.

"Can you see how many people are in there?" I asked Rob as we readied to go onstage.

"No. They've got the door closed, so no photographers can get through," he replied.

"This will be fun," Julie said, flashing her broad smile.

As we filed in I looked around at a nondescript room with brown walls and blue carpet. The décor might have been plain, but the event still seemed grand. I could feel my skin tingling with anticipation. When I stepped onstage, I was immediately blinded by camera flashes. The clicking of the cameras and the crush of reporters just a few feet away made the room feel incredibly small. I took my place beside Rob.

"Welcome, everyone," said Dr. Roland Doré, newly appointed president of the Canadian Space Agency, as he took the podium. "We're thrilled everyone can join us here today as we announce our newest class of Canadian astronauts. Ladies and gentlemen, I'm pleased to present Chris Hadfield, Julie Payette, Rob Stewart, and Dave Williams."

He waited for the applause to die down before continuing. "Please note there will be an opportunity to interview all the candidates afterwards. Let me just say that we are immensely excited about this new class of astronauts. We feel that they will do a tremendous job in representing Canada, carrying on the great work of the Canadian Space Agency, and helping to build the International Space Station."

As soon as Roland's remarks were finished, reporters rushed the stage.

"When did you decide you wanted to become an astronaut?" asked one.

"What prepared you for this moment?" demanded another.

"What can you tell us about your relationship with the other candidates?" asked a third.

We could barely answer the flurry of questions; I was still trying to convince myself the whole thing wasn't a dream.

The rest of the day was a bit of a whirlwind, and then it was time to fly back to Toronto, where with a new spring in my step I resumed my everyday life. I was still working at the hospital, and Cathy and I were making arrangements for a new chapter of our lives. But all of a sudden I'd gone from being an average person to becoming a minor celebrity— even though I'd done absolutely nothing.

"What if I don't live up to everyone's expectations?" I asked Cathy.

"Why does that concern you?" Cathy asked back. "*You* define what you consider a success."

I told myself that my first success would be to smoothly finish my remaining shifts in the emergency department. I called Tom just prior to the announcement in Ottawa to let him know that I'd gotten in. As I walked up to his office at the hospital, I couldn't help but think of everything that had happened over the past six months and whether I'd disappointed him. When the door opened, though, Tom was beaming.

"Congratulations!" he said. "When do you start?"

"Well," I said, pausing, "I have to be in Ottawa by Thursday, July 2."

"Don't worry, we'll be fine. I'll name an interim replacement and we can start the search process. Thanks for everything you've done. I'll be excited to follow your new career."

I threw myself back into my work, and my final shifts were so busy that I had little time to dwell on what might come next. In some ways I was fortunate that I had only three more weeks to work. Despite the fact that we had not yet done anything in the world of space exploration, the four of us newly named astronauts were instant celebrities. Virtually every patient I saw said, "You're that astronaut doctor, aren't you?" I knew it was getting out of hand when one patient asked me to sign the cast that I had just applied to her broken wrist. "Make sure you write 'astronaut' after your name," she said. I sheepishly obliged, assuming it wouldn't happen again, but later in that same shift another patient insisted I sign his arm.

True to the life of an emergency physician, my first shift and last shifts at Sunnybrook were night shifts, and both of them involved a surgical emergency. Years earlier, on my first shift as an emergency physician, the paramedics had brought in a twenty-eight-year-old woman with a ruptured ectopic pregnancy, a serious surgical emergency. She had no palpable pulse, but thankfully, I was able to resuscitate and stabilize her enough for a successful surgery.

My last shift was similarly chaotic. I'd been up all night seeing patients, and when I glanced at the clock behind the nurses' desk, I was shocked to see it was already 7:30 in the morning. In just thirty minutes I'd no longer be an emergency physician. I'd be an astronaut.

Ten minutes before 8:00, one of the nurses came by my desk.

"Hey, Dave," she said, "can you check on the patient in room 4? He's a young guy with abdominal pain. He's been sick a few times. I think he's got the flu. Can you examine him quickly? I need the room for somebody else."

"Sure thing," I replied. As I pulled my white lab coat on over my surgical scrubs, probably for the last time, I smiled. Before long, I'd be pulling on a space suit instead.

"Hi there, I'm Dr. Williams," I said as I entered the room. "What seems to be the problem?"

"I've been feeling nauseous and throwing up," said the young man. "It started yesterday afternoon. Earlier that day, I'd carried some heavy boxes to the car. I thought I pulled a muscle in my groin, but now I feel awful."

"All right, I'm just going to do a quick examination," I said, putting on a pair of gloves.

It was obvious he was ill. He was pale, sweating, and threw up halfway through the exam. But as I continued, the diagnosis became equally obvious. His right testicle was swollen and tender. He had a testicular torsion, a serious surgical emergency that, if not treated early, would result in permanent damage. I phoned the urology resident on call. He came down right away, confirmed the diagnosis, and scheduled the young man for emergency surgery. Thankfully, we were able to take care of the problem.

When I got home, I shared the story with Cathy.

"Lucky he had you as his doctor," Cathy said. "Doesn't that get missed sometimes?"

"It does," I said. "Sometimes it's not obvious."

"But you caught it, and everything turned out all right."

"Yes," I said. "He's fine."

Vigilance had helped me as a physician and a pilot. I hoped it would help me as an astronaut, too.

My first day of work with the Canadian Space Agency was July 2. The only thing on the agenda that day was a meet-and-greet between our training officer, the four astronauts, and our spouses. Only, it wasn't

In 1992, Mike, Chris, Julie, and I (left to right) were announced as the second class of Canadian astronauts. *Photo courtesy of NASA*

the same four of us who'd been onstage a month earlier. Rob had withdrawn his candidacy and decided to return to his work at the University of Calgary. Mike McKay, a captain in the Canadian Armed Forces, was now the fourth member of our quartet.

We gathered at R92, an old barracks in Ottawa that had served for the past few years as the home for all Canadian astronauts. The building was an old Quonset hut with squeaky floors and small, mustysmelling rooms. The offices were filled with an organized clutter of papers, files, and folders that threatened to burst off the shelves. The walls were covered with mission posters and photos of the space shuttle, the Canadarm and other memorable moments in the history of the Canadian space program.

"Check it out," I said to Cathy as we walked down the hallway for the first time. "See that poster? That's Marc Garneau's flight in '84.

And that one there—that's Roberta Bondar's mission. There's Steve's: he'll be flying on STS-52 this October." Steve MacLean, a physicist and astronaut from Ottawa who was part of Canada's first class of space explorers, was now prime crew, meaning he was on the next crew to fly in space. It was amazing how quickly we were picking up the new lingo of spaceflight.

"Your photo will be up there before long," Cathy said, squeezing my arm.

When we arrived in the meeting room, we found the entire Canadian astronaut office—the scientists, support staff, administrators—on hand to greet us. We settled in beside the others around the cramped table, with the fluorescent lights humming overhead. After a couple of minutes of small talk, the door opened, and a small man with a handlebar moustache marched in.

"Good morning, everyone. My name is Parvez Kumar, and I'm the astronaut training manager. Thank you for joining us today." He turned to Chris, Julie, Mike, and me. "I'll dive right in. Our goal today is to answer any questions you and your family might have about the program and what the next few months will bring. I know this is an exciting time and there are lots of opportunities. But you're also entering the unknown and stepping into the public eye. We want to make sure you're prepared."

Traditional, structured, and directive, Parvez had the mannerisms and bearing of a sergeant major in the British Army, right down to the accent. He had a singular, driving focus: to train the best Canadian astronauts that he could.

"We've put together a comprehensive training program similar to the one at NASA. Two of you will follow it for a year, while the other two will be selected for the NASA mission specialist class that starts in August," Parvez continued. "You've all demonstrated some level of knowledge with our Canadian space program. My goal is to prepare you to be the best astronaut, the best representative of the CSA, the best person that you can be. There is a history of distinguished astronauts who have come before you, and I intend to make sure that you continue that legacy."

I could feel my excitement building as Parvez spoke. His enthusiasm and the pride he took in the agency was infectious. I looked around the table, and everyone had the same look in their eyes: we were ready to get to work.

After our first week, Parvez called us into the conference room for a meeting.

"There have been some new developments on the NASA selection," Parvez said. You could have heard a pin drop as he paused. "Marc Garneau will be sent down as one of the mission specialists."

Each of us immediately understood that the probability of being selected to go to Houston had just decreased: only one of the four of us would get to go. The selection would be made by Bruce Aikenhead, the director general of the astronaut corps, with input from Parvez, Mac Evans, and other executives at the CSA. We were quickly getting accustomed to the ever-changing nature of human spaceflight programs.

"The three remaining astronauts will stay in Canada and participate in their own training program, which I will oversee. Don't worry, I'll keep you busy," Parvez added, as though trying to convince us that we'd be just as close to spaceflight if we stayed in Canada. It was a hard sell.

When the decision was made that Chris would join Marc as one of the first two Canadians to participate in NASA mission specialist training, I was pleased for both of them and comfortable with the decision. Chris was already living in the U.S. and was a test pilot, so he was the logical choice. I decided to focus on the positive in my situation. Despite my desire to go to Houston, I recognized that now I had time to get whatever training I needed to ensure that, when I was eventually selected for mission specialist training, I would have all the necessary skills to thrive and be at the top of my game.

I threw myself into whatever Parvez had in store for us. Calling the next few months "work" is a bit misleading. They say that when you do what you love, you'll never work a day in your life. That adage definitely applied to my training days: I'd never had so much fun. The training syllabus included gliding, skydiving, flying, scuba diving, spacecraft systems, robotic systems—it went on and on. Parvez felt it was critical that we not only get our pilot's licenses but that we were also experienced in night flying, got our instrument rating, and experienced piloting more complex single- and multiengine aircraft.

A few weeks after the selection had been made, Julie, Mike, and I went skydiving. We headed southeast of Ottawa to Embrun, Ontario, where we were to be trained by a local parachute club. I'd gone skydiving a few times before as a member of the McGill University skydiving club, so I knew the drill.

At least, that's what I thought. Parvez had briefed us on the importance of this training to get us ready for the parachute and ejection seat training we would one day receive at NASA. That rationale made a lot of sense to us. But he also had a secondary motive.

"To help you build your confidence," Parvez said, "I have asked the instructors to also teach you how to pack your own chute." I knew that the riggers who pack parachutes are highly trained, certified individuals, so this was quite the surprise.

"We're not packing our reserve chutes, are we?" I asked.

"No," Parvez responded. "They will be packed by the club's rigger, who will teach you how to pack your main chute." *Well,* I thought to myself, *if I make a mistake, at least I'll have the reserve chute.* I didn't want to be the single point failure that might lead to my own demise.

I made sure to pay particular attention to detail during the instructions. As the plane ascended, despite the beautiful view of the fields below, I couldn't help but think, *Did I untangle the lines? Did I roll the chute the way the instructor told me to?* I glanced at Julie and

Mike, wondering if they were having similar thoughts. As we neared the jump run, we checked one another's straps to make sure everything was correct.

Finally we reached the point of no return. I approached the open door of the plane, put my left foot onto the step, and reached out to grab the wing strut. It was now more dangerous to try to get back into the airplane than it was to jump. With the wind buffeting my face and body, I thought to myself, *You've done this before. This is going to be great. Now you just have to focus on enjoying the trip and forget about who packed your chute.* Needless to say, we all made it to the ground safely.

Our base for training was R-92, but as the weeks went by, our training activities often took us away from Ottawa. We traveled to Toronto for the next step of our training: high-altitude indoctrination. When flying in jet aircraft at high altitudes, it is critically important to learn how to recognize the symptoms of hypoxia—oxygen deficiency. If the aircraft pressurization systems failed, the amount of oxygen in the air we were breathing would decrease rapidly, and we could pass out if we didn't know what to watch out for.

Parvez accompanied the three of us on our trip to the Defence and Civil Institute of Environmental Medicine (DCIEM) in Toronto for the training. The institute conducted research and clinical testing for military aviation medicine and diving medicine. *Medicine and SCUBA diving in one building—I'm home,* I thought.

Dr. Gray, the military flight surgeon who oversaw our medical selection, gave us a tour of the facility and then took us to the high-altitude chamber and introduced us to the technician. The chamber was a thick-walled room with windows on both sides that sat alone in the midst of a much larger test facility. The pressure inside could be lowered to simulate the high-altitude, thin atmosphere where military jets fly. There were other chambers, too, where it could be increased to reflect the increased pressure associated with ocean dives.

"Today, you'll be going to an altitude of 40,000 feet," the technician said as we filed in. "You'll see an oxygen mask and communication headset beside your seat. Please put it on and give me a thumbs-up when you're online. Once everyone is ready, we'll start depressurizing the chamber, and I'll let you know when we reach our final altitude. When I tell you, remove your oxygen mask and start the problem sheet in front of you. Without oxygen the time of useful consciousness is typically fifteen to twenty seconds. As soon as you feel the symptoms of hypoxia, put your mask back on, go to 100 percent oxygen, and give me a thumbs-up."

The four of us relaxed in our seats. Parvez had decided to join us in the chamber to see how we reacted, and he sat beside me looking across at Julie and Mike, then back to me. I quickly snapped on the headset. No matter how many times I put one on, I always felt a sense of excitement knowing that what I was about to do was both potentially dangerous and incredibly thrilling.

I examined the paper on my clipboard and was surprised at the simplicity of the tasks. I had to write my name, solve some rudimentary math, and answer some basic questions. The first question was 20 + 36. *This shouldn't be too hard,* I thought.

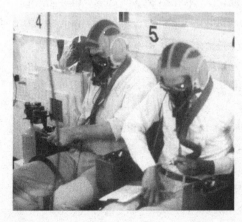

Learning how to deal with oxygen deficiency at high altitude was one of the many skills we had to acquire during our initial training. Parvez, sitting with me on his right, often joined us during our training runs.

Mike, Julie, Parvez, and I each gave the technician a thumbs-up to show we were ready. "All right, everyone," the technician's voice crackled in our headsets. "We'll be getting started in just a moment. "As we discussed, this test is going to show you the effects of hypoxia. It is not a contest. Once you feel symptoms, put your mask on right away and go to 100 percent oxygen. Any questions?"

"No," we responded in unison.

"Okay, we're going to decrease the pressure to simulate flying at 40,000 feet. Once we get to that point, we'll start the next phase."

The temperature in the chamber started to drop as the pressure decreased. The oxygen mask made breathing easy, but I could feel the hairs on my arms rise as my body responded to the colder air in the chamber. As a physician, I knew that all the gas in my body was now expanding in my ears and in my digestive tract, but I put those thoughts aside to focus on the upcoming task. *Time to be an astronaut, Dave, not a doctor. Focus on the task at hand.* It seemed pretty straightforward: Recognize the symptoms and go back on oxygen. After a few moments I heard the technician's voice over the headset.

"We're at altitude. Is everyone okay?" he asked.

"Yes," we all immediately responded.

"I'm going to ask you to remove your oxygen mask in a minute. After you remove the mask, please try to answer as many of the questions as you can. If you start to feel any of the symptoms of hypoxia—if you feel light-headed or like you might pass out—put your oxygen mask back on, go to 100 percent, and await further instructions."

The four of us traded glances. Some elementary math and an oxygen regulator? Did they really expect this exercise to be a challenge?

"All right, please remove your masks and begin," said the technician.

I took off my mask and drew a tentative breath. I was able to draw in a lungful of air, but the air was thin. I wrote my name at the top of the page and turned my attention to the math equations.

Right, 20+36, I thought. *That's obvious.* I wrote 56 as the answer. *What's next? 3 times 9. Easy—27.*

Next question. 8 + 8. No problem. 81. Wait. That doesn't seem right. No it's 16 but for some reason I wrote 81 on the page. I paused, not sure if I had made a mistake and then thought, *Hmm, the 8 looks like a vertical symbol for infinity. That's cool; it's almost like the symbol for infinity has become a rocket launching for space. That seems fitting somehow.* I turned to my left, and Parvez seemed to be contemplating a particularly complex problem that appeared off in the distance as he stared at the opposite wall. Julie and Mike had slowed down answering their questions.

Gradually, my field of vision began to shrink to a narrow cone. The doctor in me was telling me to put on my oxygen mask. *But I've got math to do,* I thought to myself, and went back to the equations. It was strange, though: I could barely see the paper. I slowly reached across the table, strapped the oxygen mask back on, and dialed it up to 100 percent. I drew a deep breath and my vision and mind immediately began to clear.

I glanced back down at the math equations. 8 + 8 = 81? What was I thinking? I turned to see how the rest of the team was doing. Julie was still looking down at her questions. Mike was back on oxygen and looked like he was trying to clear his head, and Parvez's shoulders were rising and falling rhythmically as he breathed deeply from his mask. Julie looked up and slowly put on her mask.

"Well done, everyone," said the technician. "You stayed with me! You wouldn't believe how many people lose consciousness during that test."

"How many questions were we supposed to answer?" asked Parvez. I guess he was interested in how we did.

"It doesn't matter," the technician replied. "The point is to learn your warning signs of hypoxia and recognize the first symptoms, so that if your regulator ever fails, you can descend before you lose consciousness and crash."

"So we were never supposed to finish all the questions?" Mike asked.

"Nope," said the technician.

Just like the treadmill test, I thought to myself. It's not always about winning but about staying in the game and doing what needs to get done.

"We're going to rapidly repressurize now," the tech continued. With that, hazy fog flooded into the room as the temperature climbed. Parvez, Mike, and Julie were quickly enveloped in the mist; within seconds, I could barely see them. As the pressure in the room increased, the air compressed our ears; it felt like we were descending underwater for a scuba dive. It would be fun explaining this to Cathy, who was now flying the Airbus A320.

Every moment of training was both immensely challenging and incredibly entertaining. Not a day went by that I didn't laugh and smile at some strange new experience. Still, I recognized that on some level this was work. Throughout the first few months of our training, Parvez and the other CSA officials were constantly evaluating our performance and reviewing the feedback we received from our various instructors.

Our training continued to take us across the country as we visited Canadian space companies and research facilities. We did geology training in Sudbury, where we learned how to differentiate impact craters from volcanic ones. We had lectures on earth observation, oceanography, and planetary science. We learned about performance psychology training and how to use mental imagery as a tool to practice physical tasks. I had finished my night flying training and was now well into my multiengine rating and preparing for my commercial pilot's license. It was a constant learning process, one that followed me home each night.

"What are you reading?" Cathy asked one night as she glanced at my textbook.

"A Russian language tutorial," I replied, rubbing my tired eyes.

"Will you be speaking Russian on the space station?"

"*Da,*" I responded.

Cathy took another sidelong glance at the textbook. "Better you than me."

One of the highlights of our training that year was flying in the KC-135, affectionately known as the Vomit Comet. In space, our job as astronauts would be to successfully conduct science experiments in a zero-gravity environment. The only way to simulate that was to fly endless parabolas on the Vomit Comet to get used to performing tasks and using tools while floating weightless.

"The principle behind the KC-135 is simple," Parvez explained to us in our office before we flew to Houston for our training and first set of flights. "The plane will fly a series of parabolas, almost like riding waves, as it climbs from 24,000 to 34,000 feet." I imagined a roller coaster without the restraints. "When the plane gets to 34,000 feet, the pilots will push the aircraft into a steep dive, and you'll experience roughly twenty seconds of weightlessness. When the plane gets back to 24,000 feet, there's a 2-g pullout as the aircraft climbs back to repeat the sequence. We will repeat this process approximately forty times."

I looked over and caught Julie grinning. Mike looked similarly enthusiastic.

"Try not to get sick, as you'll be helping the investigators with their experiments," Parvez continued. "If they get sick, you may need to finish the work for them." Parvez was never one to beat around the bush. "I suggest taking the antinausea medication they offer. It helps."

We all flew to Houston the next week for four days of flying. Our first briefing was at 8:00 a.m. on Monday morning and we arrived the day before. We checked into the hotel, and since this was my first time visiting Johnson Space Center as an astronaut, I headed straight for the Outpost Tavern.

Originally a U.S. Air Force barracks near Ellington Field, the building had changed hands a couple of times before it was moved closer to Johnson Space Center and opened as the Outpost in 1981. It quickly became a regular hangout for astronauts and NASA staff. It is generally not a good idea to go out drinking the night before a KC-135 flight, so, as excited as I was, I limited myself to one beer and left early to get some sleep.

Bob Williams, the test director for the KC-135, who'd flown more than 71,000 parabolas, greeted us at the briefing the next morning. We reviewed the safety procedures, and Bob shared insights into how to move around gracefully in microgravity and, more importantly, how to position ourselves for the pullout so we didn't come crashing down to the floor from the ceiling of the plane.

"If you're worried about getting sick, I'd strongly suggest you take the scop-dex medication and keep a barf bag readily available in your flight suit pocket," he said.

Parvez passed around little paper cups with two pills in them. I peered into the cup and recognized one (scopolamine) as an anti-nausea pill and the other (dextroamphetamine; brand name Dexedrine) as a stimulant to offset the drowsiness. There was a moment of hesitation in the group as we looked at each other. *Do we need to take this?* we were all thinking. *Who thinks they can go without it and tough it out?* I thought of all the ups and downs of the trip and decided it was better to save my stomach than my face. I had no problem taking the scopolamine to combat the nausea, but I left the Dexedrine in the cup. Dexedrine is also known as speed, and I wasn't sure how I'd react to it. I figured I could deal with any drowsiness the antinausea pill brought on.

Once again, Parvez joined us on the front lines of our training. He had flown on the KC-135 before and seemed genuinely excited to share our first exposure to microgravity with us.

The inside of the plane was lined with closed-cell foam padding, similar to the wrestling mats we'd used in our high school gym classes. The smell defied description: a blend of old airplane mixed with a hint of foam and a mild whiff of old vomit. Bob had told us that some people get nauseous as soon as they got on board. *I can believe it,* I thought as I breathed deeply through my mouth.

We strapped in and the plane taxied for takeoff. Stephanie Wells, one of the NASA aircraft operations division pilots, was in command. A former U.S. Air Force pilot, Stephanie was known for the quality of her parabolas.

Once we had entered the test area above the Gulf of Mexico, we got out of our seats and stood in the cabin holding overhead straps to maintain our balance.

"Get ready," Bob yelled above the aircraft noise. "We're going to start the first pull-up."

I lay down on the floor as the g-forces rapidly increased. Then the sound of the engines changed as the aircraft nosed over into the steep dive. I floated gracefully off the floor and seemed to hover in midair. I felt like a beached fish trying to flop my way toward a handhold. Bob gave me a push in the direction of the experiment that I was to assist with, and just like that my microgravity science career started.

There were a few issues to contend with as the parabolas continued. Despite the air-conditioning, the vomit smell of the cabin got even more pungent. Mike, Julie, and I distracted ourselves with our experiments, trying to make sure our instruments didn't float away during the descents. Meanwhile, Parvez floated around with a big smile on his face, watching how things were progressing. Before I knew it, we'd flown our last parabola. We then strapped into our seats for the ride back to the air base.

After we landed, Bob asked, "Who's up for some Cajun barbecue? Pe-Te's is right across the street."

Julie, Mike, and I were game, but a number of the others didn't seem particularly interested. I later learned that among NASA personnel, the real proof of a lead stomach was being able to fly in the morning, have lunch at Pe-Te's, and then fly again in the afternoon.

In late October, we took a break from our training for a road trip. It was a special occasion: Steve MacLean was going to be launching on STS-52, a ten-day mission orbiting the earth. Parvez wanted us to be at the launch to witness the latest Canadian astronaut head into space. Chris and Marc were still in ASCAN training, but Mike, Julie, and I headed down to Florida.

The morning of the launch, I stood with all the other spectators at the Banana Creek viewing site looking across the water at the launchpad, now much smaller in the distance. Friends, family, and onlookers were gathered to cheer on the astronauts. I brought my video camera so I could record every moment of that launch.

"Imagine what it must look like from up there," Mike said, his camera at the ready as the countdown clock continued.

"I suppose their view is pretty limited," I said. "I wonder what we'll be thinking about when we're up there."

Smiles spread across Mike's and Julie's faces.

"One day that will be us," I said.

I closed my eyes. What would it be like on that shuttle during the final stages of countdown? Instead of a warm sea breeze, cool air would be pumping through my suit. In place of the chatter of the crowd, I'd have Mission Control in my ear. And instead of looking at the green and blue horizon, I'd soon be staring straight up into the sky. I couldn't wait!

Finally, the moment arrived. The launch preparations were complete, and loudspeakers with the voice of a NASA representative could be heard counting down. "Ten, nine, eight—we have a go for main engine start—five, four, three, two, one, zero. We have ignition . . . and liftoff." The crowd applauded and cheers of "Go, Steve, go!" rose up around us as the solid rocket boosters roared to life, spewing the water from the suppression system into vapor under the shuttle. I could feel the ground shaking from the engines bellowing to life three miles away. My shirt vibrated gently from the force of it. *Columbia* rocketed into the sky.

As I watched the shuttle shrink to a distant speck, I thought about my own journey. What lay ahead for me? There were still twists and turns, but on that incredible day, literally and figuratively, everything was looking up.

7

Space Medicine and the Funky Chicken

Commitment demands two things: patience and sacrifice. In the summer of 1993, we were learning a lot about both. The astronaut office moved out of the military hut in Ottawa to a brand-new Canadian Space Agency building in Montréal, which meant that Cathy and I had to move as well. Cathy had five years of experience as an Air Canada pilot but was on a temporary layoff that affected a number of their pilots.

We moved back to the West Island of Montréal, close to where I grew up. The creek and woods that I had explored as a child were still there, albeit smaller now thanks to the new housing developments.

"What's next in the training program?" Cathy asked as we unpacked the last of our things in our new home.

"Good question," I said, taking a model of the Avro Arrow out of a box. "I think we'll be given collateral duty assignments while we continue our training."

"And what does that mean in English?"

"They're our day jobs for the next few months while we continue with the next round of training and wait for an assignment to a mission specialist class with NASA."

On my first day in the new office, Frank Vigneron, the new head of the astronaut corps after Bruce's retirement, called me into his office.

"Dave, I've seen how excited you are about space medicine. I'd like you to set up an operational space medicine program within the astronaut office," Frank said, leaning back in his office chair.

I answered without hesitation. "Amazing! I've been hoping that we'd be able to start working on this. There will be a lot to do to get ready for medical care on the space station. Will we have a budget?"

Frank smiled. "I knew you'd ask that. Let me have a look and see what I can do. What exactly are you thinking?"

"I think Canada should play a role. NASA has an entire space medicine team at Johnson Space Center. We should have the same capability up here. We could even partner and collaborate with institutes across the country that are already working in this field."

Frank stared at me over the rims of his glasses. I started to sweat. Why wasn't he speaking? Was my vision too bold? I wasn't even an official astronaut yet. Who was I to be proposing major initiatives?

"All right," Frank finally said. "Let's do it."

Shortly after that meeting, I was named the manager of the newly minted CSA operational space medicine program. On paper, it seemed very impressive. In practice, it meant taking on much more responsibility in addition to my regular training. The team included Patrick Sullivan, Leena Tomi, Natalie Hirsch, and a graduate student, Carrie Olha. I was excited: we had the team, a vision, and now a mandate to focus on the clinical care of Canadian astronauts.

Soon after I started in my new role, Frank sent me down to Johnson Space Center for a meeting with the NASA space medicine team. The trip opened my eyes to how far we could push human limits in space and what the space program might accomplish. Space exploration had already led us to breakthroughs in everything from insulin delivery to cancer treatments and ultrasound techniques. Now we would be focusing on developing new technologies and clinical protocols to manage the health care of astronauts on long duration missions to the space station.

I met with Dr. Roger Billica, head of the space medicine branch at Johnson Space Center, and it quickly became clear that NASA had a vision that they were rapidly turning into reality. They were developing a new crew health care system and already envisioned an international collaboration to develop and assess new medical technologies and protocols. I was impressed.

Roger went on to describe the Multinational Space Medicine Board, an international group of flight surgeons who would oversee medical certification of astronauts and cosmonauts assigned to missions to the International Space Station. That same board would later manage tourists visiting the space station. *Tourist trips to space,* I thought. *If only Dad could hear this.*

On top of that, there would be a second, ultimate authority for health care on the ISS—the Multinational Medical Policy Board. It had not yet been formed but would be put in place prior to sending the first crew mission to the ISS. Little did I know, I would later be the first cochair of that board with Dr. Anatoly Grigoriev of the Institute of Biomedical Problems in Russia.

My visit illustrated how much was already under way, but I also saw that there was an opportunity for collaboration. I was sorry to leave Houston, but the trip confirmed Frank's and my shared belief that Canada had a role to play in space medicine. I marveled at what our new program in Canada might help accomplish.

We quickly brought the space medicine program forward by leaps and bounds. I had to keep up my astronaut training in the meantime, though, which made for long days and nights.

"Dave, can you please move your suture kit off the dining room table?" Cathy asked one evening.

"Sorry. We're practicing suturing on the Falcon 20 tomorrow, and I was just getting the flight kit ready," I said.

"Sounds fun. But maybe you can put it somewhere else? It's hard to set the table when it looks like the emergency room."

As our flight training continued, Parvez felt that it was time to step things up a notch.

"You're going to be doing aerobatic flight training and I want each of you to be completely comfortable with g-forces," he said looking at Julie, Mike, and me during one of our morning briefings. "Next week we will go back to the DCIEM for centrifuge training to get you ready for the g-forces you'll experience flying the NASA T-38 and during the shuttle launch."

When we arrived at the DCIEM, an instructor was waiting for us.

"Welcome back," he said, shaking our hands and leading us inside.

"There won't be any math questions this time, will there?" I asked as we passed the altitude chamber we'd visited a few months prior.

"Not this time," the instructor said with a smile. "Today your goal is simple: Don't lose consciousness."

Simple doesn't mean easy, I thought.

The instructor led us to a control room overlooking a large circular room with a concrete floor and white walls that wouldn't have been out of place in a generic warehouse. In the middle of the room sat the centrifuge itself: a long metal frame with a cockpit on one end and a counterweight on the other, anchored to a motor.

"Normally, we'd have you wearing a g-suit when you spin. But the aerobatic airplanes you will be flying and the T-38 are not set up for g-suits, so we want you to know what you're dealing with," he explained. "It is important to learn how to properly do a g-straining maneuver. If you feel like you're going to faint, let go of the dead man's switch and the centrifuge will stop. I'll do the first run to show you what to do."

The instructor hopped into the capsule-shaped crew compartment and showed us how to attach the five-point restraint.

"You have to bend your boom mike up a bit, as it'll be pulled down by the g-forces," he said as he put on his communications cap, a cloth headset helmet. "We won't wear regular helmets because even the lightweight ones are pretty heavy when you're pulling 5 g's; a ten-pound helmet would be like a fifty-pound weight on your head. Most aerobatics pilots just wear a cloth helmet or lightweight headset."

We went back to the control room and gathered around a screen displaying the cockpit camera.

"Let's begin," he said, his voice crackling over the speakers.

An operator flicked a few switches in the control room beside us and the machine began to slowly rotate around its center.

"The thing you need to remember in the g-strain maneuver is to tighten your abs after taking a deep breath," the instructor said. "You need to keep the blood flowing to your head so you don't pass out."

The crew compartment started to whip past the window a little faster, but the instructor didn't stop talking.

"When you need to breathe," he said, his voice getting tighter, "exhale a little, breathe in fully, then tighten your muscles."

I looked over to the monitor: it had climbed to 5.5 g's. The flight surgeon's eyes looked like they were bulging out of their sockets as he performed his anti-g maneuver.

"And remember—"

His voice cut off suddenly as his eyes rolled back and his limbs started seizing and twitching involuntarily.

"That's not good," Julie said.

"Is he okay?" Mike asked.

"He'll be fine," said the control operator as he brought the machine to a stop. "He just g-LOC'd" (experienced loss of consciousness from g-forces). Inside the crew compartment, our instructor was slowly regaining consciousness. "Most people do the funky chicken when they pass out in the centrifuge," the control operator added, shrugging nonchalantly.

When he was finally reoriented, our instructor unbuckled himself, stepped out of the crew compartment, and turned to see all of us looking at him in concern.

"Don't do what I just did," he advised sheepishly. "Don't try to talk too much while you're straining. You've just seen it doesn't work. You'll find that staying conscious is preferable to the alternative.

"Dave," he said. "You're up first."

Oh, boy, I thought. *Time to avoid doing what he just did.*

I walked toward the centrifuge and climbed into the crew compartment, where I buckled myself in. *Focus, be alert . . . This will be just like the g-forces in the airplane,* I told myself. *Tighten, force, and breathe . . . tighten, force, and breathe.*

"Are you ready?" the control operator asked over the headset.

"Yes," I replied, adjusting my mike higher just in case.

"Remember, this isn't a contest. Let go of the switch when you feel your vision starting to tunnel."

"Copy," I said. I was feeling a little anxious and excited at the same time. I had made it through life so far without doing the funky chicken; I didn't want to start today.

The machine kicked to life beneath me. Each second the g-forces got heavier and heavier. As the crushing force pushed me down into my seat, my field of vision got smaller and smaller. I strained my core muscles as hard as I could, building the pressure in my chest. At the same time I contracted the muscles in my legs with all my strength, and my vision returned to normal. *This really works,* I thought. The centrifuge went faster, 6 g's, 7 g's, then 7.2. Bit by bit, my vision decreased into a narrow cone. I released the kill switch and the centrifuge started to slow.

Hold it, Dave, hold it! I kept repeating in my head. If I stopped

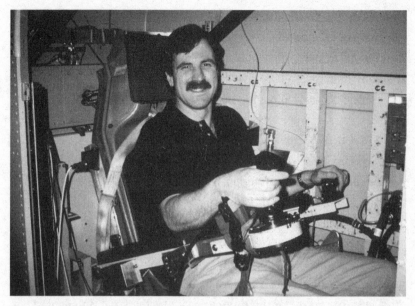

The cockpit of the centrifuge looked and felt similar to the ones in planes I'd flown before. Of course, that was before the g-forces kicked in.

straining now, I'd still risk losing consciousness as the centrifuge slowed to a stop.

Finally, the machine shuddered to a halt. "All right, the warm-up is done," the instructor said. "Ready to start the real thing?"

He was joking, thankfully. It was over. I hadn't lost consciousness, vomited, or otherwise embarrassed myself. And I'd managed to escape the funky chicken. A good start. I walked slowly to the exit, my muscles aching from the exertion.

The interest in space medicine was growing within the astronaut office, so I decided it was time to chat with Frank again about our program. While there had been three Canadian missions on the space shuttle, we had no long-duration flight experience aboard a space station. The ISS construction had not started yet, so that meant a long-term Canadian mission would have to be on *Mir*, the Russian space station. I ran the idea by Dr. Bob Thirsk, the only other Canadian physician astronaut, and he agreed it would be a fantastic opportunity.

"Frank," I said, knocking on his office door. "Do you have a minute?"

"Of course, Dave," he said. "What's on your mind?"

I explained my plan.

Frank immediately asked, "What would it cost?"

I swallowed: it was the question I'd been dreading. "Typically it's around $1 million U.S. a day," I said.

Frank paused, considering. "Let me think about it further," he said. "In the meantime, see if you can get some more information on what resources would be required."

Over the course of the summer of 1993, the space medicine team worked hard to get ready for a visit to Moscow in early September. Frank came through for us, and he decided that if we were successful he would recommend to senior management that Bob would fly the mission and that I would be his backup. I had no problem with that. Within a year of being hired, I was now part of a team planning a long-duration mission to the *Mir* space station. I was thrilled.

The day that I left, Cathy hugged me good-bye. "Have a great trip. Love you," she said, standing in the doorway of our house at West Island.

"See you in a week," I responded. "Love you, too."

It was a twelve-hour flight to Moscow, but there was a stopover in Paris. We arrived early Sunday evening. The next morning we met the Russian team in the hotel lobby. One of our team members, Leena Tomi, spoke to them in fluent Russian. Born in Finland, Leena had studied in St. Petersburg before coming to Canada to do a master's degree in aerospace physiology at McGill.

I noticed there were a number of smiling faces and a few laughs as the members of the Russian team looked at me. I asked Leena quietly, "Are they talking about me? What are they saying?"

"You're a big guy. They don't think you'll fit in the Soyuz spacecraft," she said with a smile. "Bob will, but they're not so sure about you."

They were right. Later that week we definitively learned I did not fit in the standard Soyuz spacecraft seat. But it didn't matter. The cost turned out to be simply too much for our budget, and shortly after our trip, NASA signed an agreement to send American astronauts to the *Mir* space station, which also included a seat redesign for larger astronauts.

We were disappointed, given how much preparation we'd done, so we headed home to regroup. A few weeks later I was back with our space medicine team. We brainstormed what we could do to get some experience in space medicine.

"What if we did a simulated mission?" Pat suggested. "We could use the DCIEM facilities."

The response was a unanimous "Great idea!"

Frank was completely supportive, and within a week we had a plan. We would set up a one-week simulated spaceflight in a hyperbaric chamber at DCIEM. Bob would serve as the commander, and Julie, Mike, and I would be his crew. Throughout the mission, we'd conduct space medicine experiments that we received from Canadian and international researchers. It wasn't the same as flying on *Mir*, but it was better than nothing.

We entered the chamber on February 7, 1994, and closed the hatch at 9:00 a.m. The chamber would not be pressurized, but we had agreed that once the hatch was closed, it would stay closed for the entire week.

"Just like on board a space station," Julie said after we were settled.

"Minus the weightlessness," Mike added.

One of our first experiments was to record brain wave activity. I was quite familiar with EEG recordings from my graduate studies, so I was the first subject. I looked over the checklist and saw that it called for gel to be applied to the electrodes. *I know exactly what to do,* I thought.

I turned to the supply shelf, but the gel wasn't stowed where it was supposed to be. I called Pat, the equivalent of a capsule communicator in our mission control, over the radio. "Pat, I can't find the EEG gel where it was supposed to be stowed. Do you have any insight on where else I should look?"

"Stand by," Pat answered. A couple of minutes later Pat came on again. "Dave, there was an oversight and the gel didn't get stowed. Can you figure out a workaround?"

"Let me see what I can do," I responded.

The purpose of electrode gel is improve the conductivity of the electrical signal from the scalp to the electrode. *Maybe if I mix table salt with Vaseline I can put together a concoction that would work,* I thought.

"Bob, is it okay if I use some of our table salt?" I asked, heading into the galley.

"Sure," he said, looking up from his crew notebook. "Hungry already?"

"Not yet. Making a workaround," I answered.

"Okay, let me know how it goes."

After smearing my homemade gel onto the electrodes and attaching them to my scalp, I checked that the signal was usable and proceeded with the experiment. It went off without another hitch, and the rest of the week passed without the need for further kitchen science experiments.

After a full week in a chamber, I was glad when that hatch opened and I could go back home. "Welcome back," Cathy said as I walked in the house.

"Thanks," I said.

"How did it go?"

"We had to get a bit creative at times, but all in all I'd say it was a success."

"That's great."

"How have you been?" I asked.

Cathy smiled and then shared some fantastic news.

"Dave, I'm pregnant," Cathy said.

"That's amazing!" I said. I was overflowing with happiness: I couldn't believe how fortunate I was. One of the first things we did was trade our Nissan 300ZX sports car for a Pathfinder to make room for the new addition to our family.

We spent the next few months getting ready for the birth of our first child. We'd meet up in the evenings after work and shop for a car seat or look at cribs. My mother had already been sending diapers, bottles, and toys. Our inventory of baby-related paraphernalia was growing daily.

Finally, on a muggy evening in late August 1994, I got the call.

"Dave, it's time," Cathy said. "I'm packing my bag for the hospital."

I dropped everything. "I'll be right there," I said.

I raced home to pick up Cathy and then we sped to the delivery room. I was still getting used to going to hospitals as a patient rather than as a doctor. My former work attire of scrubs and white coat had been replaced by khakis, polo shirts, and flight suits, but on this particular occasion those thoughts were far from my head.

We made it in time and everything went well. Cathy was amazing. When the doctor finally handed us our baby boy, I was overjoyed. We couldn't stop smiling as Cathy held him close. "Here, you hold him," she said.

As I took our son in my arms, I marveled at how incredible childbirth was. Here was a beautiful baby boy and already I was envisioning tossing a ball together, going camping, and doing all of the things I had enjoyed doing with my own dad. I wanted to be the best father possible.

Looking at his body in my arms, the doctor in me took over. Even though he wasn't crying and seemed perfectly content to be in my arms, something wasn't quite right. But I didn't focus on that. I was caught up with how incredible he was.

"What should we name him?" I asked.

"I like Evan," Cathy replied.

"Me, too."

The nurses bustled around us, clearing the room so we could have some quiet time together. About an hour after the delivery, we were back in Cathy's room with Evan asleep in her arms, and the doctor returned.

"Dr. and Mrs. Williams," he said, "there's no easy way to say this. I'm afraid that Evan has Down syndrome. We'll have the neonatologist have a look at him to be sure, and we'll need to send off some tests."

"What kind of tests?" Cathy asked.

"Just standard blood work and analysis we do after every birth to make sure the baby is otherwise healthy. But we'll have to add a genetic screening test."

I felt a blow to my gut. Every parent wants the best for their child and for them to have an easy life. It seemed like the cards were stacked against Evan right from the start.

Over the next few days we met with doctors and nurses to learn more about Down syndrome and how to prepare for this new chapter of our lives. Years before, I had volunteered at a school for children with special needs and studied the condition as a medical professional, but this was different. This was far more real and personal than any textbook lesson. Genetics and cell biology were of little help to me.

"We're going to get through this, " Cathy reassured me.

There were times between us when words weren't enough, but as always I knew we were in this together. We resolved to find our way through.

"You'll want to look into respite care," one professional gently told us before we left the hospital.

Cathy and I exchanged a confused look.

"Sorry, why would we need respite care?" I asked.

The man clasped his hands in front of him. "Some parents find that they need a break or extra support when taking care of a child with extra needs."

We responded together. "That won't be necessary."

"Evan is our son," I added. "We won't need a break from him." Our goal was to raise Evan just as we would have if he didn't have special needs. We still saw a future in which we would toss the football around, play basketball, and even ski together. Why focus on limits? As we headed home from the hospital, we thought only of the good things that would come, and how we'd let Evan help us figure out what those limits might be.

8

NASA Training and the Slugs

In November 1994, I arrived at the CSA office on a blustery winter morning. I'd barely stomped the snow off my shoes and sat down at my desk when I got a call.

"Dave, it's Mac." I froze. William MacDonald Evans—or Mac Evans, as we called him—was now the president of the Canadian Space Agency. If he was calling, something big was afoot. "Can you come up to my office?"

"I'll be right there," I said.

I raced up to Mac's office, wondering what he needed to talk about so urgently. *Maybe they've decided to cut the space medicine program? But surely Frank would have told me if that happened . . .*

I arrived at Mac's office to find him standing in front of his desk.

"What's up, Mac?" I asked.

"Nothing at all, Dave. In fact, I have good news. NASA has se-lected their next class of mission specialists, and I'm delighted to say you're one of them."

I broke into a wide smile. It had been a very busy couple of weeks, with a number of challenges, and any good news was welcome. "Mac, that's incredible. Thanks very much!"

"Incredible, for sure. It's a great day for you and for the program."

"When do I start?"

"You'll report to Houston in March, so you have a bit of time to prepare."

I felt as though I were floating above the ground. *It's finally hap-pening,* I thought to myself. *I can't wait to tell Cathy. But wait . . .* With that, my head began to clear. I had so many questions, and I now had new priorities. There was one truly important thing I needed to ask.

"Mac, if I move to Houston, will the agency help with special needs care for Evan?"

"Of course, Dave. You can count on that. We can sort out the de-tails, but we'll make sure your family has everything they need."

I went straight back to my office to call Cathy.

"I'll dig out the moving boxes," she said with a laugh.

We weren't able to find a house before we moved down south, so for the first couple of weeks in Houston we lived in a small, one-bed hotel room while we looked for a rental. I was nervously preparing for my first day. Meanwhile, Cathy was trying to figure out how best to manage her new commute between Houston and Toronto. She had been recalled and was now training on the Airbus A320. We were both exhausted and stressed. But not Evan. He was then as he is now: always in a good mood, ready for something fun.

We finally found a house and moved in at the beginning of May. Evan loved scooting around in his walker, a huge smile on his face as he explored his new play space. Despite the long days and the busy training schedule, it was great to come home in the evening to be with Cathy and Evan. Often as I read one of the many training manuals on space shuttle systems, he'd fall asleep on my chest. He was particularly fond of the red Snowbirds flight suit that we had gotten for him, appropriate attire for the son of two pilots. Cathy and I were both so thankful for Evan. He always brought us back. It was Evan who kept us grounded.

Monday, March 6, finally rolled around, and with it a massive rainstorm. I turned on the radio as I made coffee that morning, just in time to catch the station host listing the events and services that would be closed because of the rain. The whole city was a mess.

I can't be late on my first day, I thought as I grabbed the car keys. *Besides, it's just rain.*

The rain was pooling in the street, but I figured our SUV could handle it. I headed down Space Center Boulevard toward Johnson Space Center. At every intersection I passed, the water rose a little higher. Before long, it reached the base of my car door. When I got to Bay Area Boulevard, the intersection was completely underwater. I looked for a way around it. That's when I saw a man canoeing down the street in the opposite direction. Maybe I was going to be late after all.

I eventually made it to Johnson Space Center, found building 4 South, and went to the meeting room in the astronaut office on the sixth floor. It wasn't exactly the grand entrance I had envisioned. It looked like I had taken a shower with my clothes on, and my feet squelched as I entered the room. I took my seat at the back of the room beside an older man who was equally disheveled.

"Just a little wet out there, eh?" I said.

"I could barely get my car through it," he replied in a French accent.

"I'm Dave." I extended my hand.

"Jean-Loup," he said as we shook.

I recognized the name: Jean-Loup Chrétien was a general in the

French air force. He had already flown in space with the Russians. Jean-Loup turned and spoke in rapid French to the man beside him, who was also a test pilot from the French air force. When the last of us finally filed in, Duane Ross, the head of the astronaut selection office, walked to the center of the room.

"Welcome aboard," Duane said. "We have some briefings this morning, starting with Bob Cabana, the head of the Astronaut Office. Your class photo is scheduled for 1300 in building 9. Hopefully it won't be raining as hard at that point, or you might have a memorable photo. We'll have to call you the Wet Slugs."

"The Slugs" was the class name given to us by the preceding 1992 class, "the Hogs."

"But before we get started," Duane continued, "let's go around the room and introduce ourselves."

We each took our turn to stand and speak. There were only four of us from outside the United States. Jean-Loup was from the CNES (Centre national d'études spatiales, or National Center for Space Studies), France's space program, and the European Space Agency, as was his fellow countryman Michel Tognini. Takao Doi, an astronaut from the Japanese space agency, the National Space Development Agency of Japan, and I were the remaining two. The other nineteen astronauts were American.

"Welcome to all of our international friends and to all of you who are joining us from out of town. We're looking forward to starting your training. I'd like to introduce your training manager, Paige Maultsby. Paige will be coordinating your ASCAN training."

Paige rose to great us. "I'm looking forward to getting to know each of you," she said. "As you're getting settled, if there is anything you need, don't hesitate to come and ask. We're all here to help."

The rest of the morning was a whirlwind. Bob Cabana spoke to us about our ASCAN year, the opportunity for future shuttle flights, and the many space walks that would be required to build the International

Space Station. "It will be an exciting time for all of you. Welcome aboard." After he finished, Paige stood up to address our group again.

"I have a list of your offices. You'll find a number of training materials already on your desk with this week's schedule. Most important, you'll find a copy of *The Shuttle Crew Operations Manual* and the T-38 Dash 1 manual. After the photo session today, you need to go to Ellington to be sized for your boots and helmets. I'll be in my office if you need me."

I went to my new office on the fifth floor and found my desk. *The Shuttle Crew Operations Manual* was a four-inch-thick binder with a picture on the cover of the shuttle lifting off. The manual was an overview of all the shuttle systems, each of which would have further stacks of system-specific training materials. The T-38 manual was slim by comparison—only two inches thick—and was accompanied by a checklist with the ground school and flight training syllabus. I looked at my schedule for the rest of the week and saw that we were diving right in over the first few days: a tour of JSC, a swim test at a local swimming pool, and a series of lectures on orbiter systems.

Looks like I've got some late nights ahead of me, I thought as I flipped through the hundreds of pages.

The early days of our training in Houston closely resembled what I'd done in Canada: ejection seat training, parachute landings, survival training, briefings on the different NASA centers, and meetings with our strength and conditioning coaches at the gym. There were some minor variations to what I had experienced with Parvez. One of the most surprising changes was that there would be written exams for our system training. We were the first astronaut class to have official written tests. Nobody ever asked what would happen if we didn't pass—because none of us wanted to find out.

For every minute in the classroom, we spent one in the simulator to make sure we could apply what we'd learned. Before we could start using the simulators, though, we had to learn what they were for and where they were located. As ASCANs, most of our time was spent in the single-system trainers where we learned the shuttle systems. Every now and then we'd change things up with an ascent or entry simulation in the motion simulator or an orbit simulation in the fixed-base trainer. As our training progressed, we realized that for everything we would do in space, NASA had developed a simulator for us to use for practice on Earth. That included the shuttle toilet, also known as the waste containment system, which I was surprised to see had its own training session in the schedule.

So much of the training at NASA was based on one simple premise: getting us ready for spaceflight. We were constantly pushing our limits, learning everything we had to know to succeed. It was like drinking from a firehose for the duration of our ASCAN training. As we learned to depend on one another in the simulators and the T-38, our camaraderie and team spirit grew.

One of the biggest challenges for the nonpilot astronauts was to fly the T-38 supersonic jets. NASA used those specific aircraft for spaceflight readiness training because they demanded the same skills that we would ultimately need in space: teamwork, situational awareness, multitasking, and concise communication. Plus, compared to civilian aircraft, the T-38 went really fast.

The first time I approached the plane on the runway, I felt a mixture of emotions, from excitement to awe to respect, then fear. Making a mistake at Mach 0.95 could have catastrophic consequences, but making one in space at Mach 25 would be far worse. It was a clear spring day in April—perfect weather for my first syllabus flight. Even sitting on the ground, the T-38 looked fast. Its razor-sharp wings and pointed nose seemed poised to slice through the air. Walking across the tarmac to the plane, it was hard not to hear the theme music from *Top Gun* or *The Right Stuff* in my head.

"I've never flown in a supersonic jet before," I told the pilot.

"You're in for a treat," he said. For him, this was just another ASCAN IP hop—or an astronaut candidate instructor-pilot flight. For me, it was my first exposure to the world of high-performance aviation and supersonic flight.

As we walked to the plane, my skin tingled. With all my flight training and studying, I felt prepared, but I was still a little nervous. The instructor sensed my hesitation.

"How many flying hours have you logged?" he asked.

"About four hundred. I have a commercial license with a multi-engine rating and I'm halfway through my instrument training," I said.

"That's great!"

His enthusiasm was meant to calm me down.

"Let's do the walkaround," he said, and proceeded to show me everything on the aircraft that needed to be checked before we climbed into the cockpit.

I settled into the back seat. The ground crew watched me fasten my five-point harness to make sure I had done it correctly.

"Comm check," the instructor said over the radio.

"I have you five by five, how me?" I responded, using the concise approach to communication that was part of my flight training.

"I have you loud and clear," he said.

Together, we ran through the preflight checklist strapped to my leg. The stories of unfortunate back seaters who'd inadvertently lost a map or piece of paper into the engines had already circulated among our class. We all knew of the dangers of unrestrained objects in the back seat of a plane with an open canopy on a windy day.

"Ready for engine start?" the instructor asked.

"Yes," I said, double-checking for loose papers.

We taxied into takeoff position, and what seemed like only a couple of seconds later the afterburner kicked in and we roared down the runway. It felt like my brain had been left behind. It was the fastest I'd ever moved before. It was as if I had blinked, and suddenly we were at 10,000 feet.

"Wow, that's impressive," I said after acknowledging the radio handoff between controllers. No wonder this thing was called the White Rocket.

"That's most people's reaction on their first flight," my pilot said.

"I'm going to take us out over the water to the training area," he continued, setting a course to the southwest.

The view was incredible. I could see the Gulf of Mexico stretching out to the horizon, the ships dotting its surface mere specks beneath us.

"Are you ready to go supersonic?"

"Sure," I said, trying to quiet the seven-year-old me cheering and jumping up and down in my seat.

"You can add a little power and drop the nose a bit. And watch the airspeed," he said.

I tilted the plane's nose into a shallow dive, and I watched the Mach meter climb: 0.95, 0.97, 0.99. I braced myself for a boom or for the plane to shake, but nothing happened. The meter hit Mach 1.0 then 1.1 and, just like that, we were supersonic. I was amazed at how smooth it was. I recalled the scenes from the movie *The Right Stuff* that showed how difficult it had been to achieve supersonic flight and inwardly thanked the aerospace engineers who designed the T-38. I pulled out of the dive and the airspeed dropped back to Mach 0.99.

"Pull the throttles back to 88 percent and we'll slow down for some air work," the instructor said. "We'll start with level flight and then do some turns." Once we had finished all the training objectives he said, "All right, time for a little fun."

"What kind of fun?" I asked.

"Ever done a loop or an aileron roll?"

Thank goodness for Parvez and his insistence that we do aerobatic training. "Sure," I said. I've always found loops easy. Pull the stick back, keep the wings level and don't pull more than 5 g's as you look back over your head to complete the loop. Aileron rolls are a little different. You pull the nose up slightly and rotate the plane in a constant rolling maneuver around its longitudinal axis while it continues to fly forward. The 720-degree-per-second roll rate of the T-38 can make this a disorienting maneuver, especially if you hold full-stick deflection for a couple of seconds.

"You have control. Pull back smoothly and keep an eye on the g-forces," he said.

I pulled back as the g-forces built gradually to 5 g's in the loop. I was crushed down in my seat with my helmet now feeling as though it were a twenty-five-pound weight on my head. It was an interesting paradox trying to fly smoothly while straining to stay conscious and being crushed in my seat. Pulling out of the loop, I leveled off and handed control back to the instructor.

"You have control," I said, pushing the stick forward and backward.

"Thanks," he said. "Let's do some rolls." He pushed the stick as far as it would go to the left. My head snapped right and the ride began.

"That roll rate is pretty impressive!" I said as we finished the sequence of four rolls in a row in two seconds. "If we keep this up, I think I'm going to be sick."

My pilot chuckled as he eased off the rolls. I exhaled as we settled back into level flight.

Then I asked, "Do you mind if I take the controls again?"

"Sure, no problem."

I took the stick and immediately started us back into a series of aileron rolls. I didn't feel sick now that I was in control. After repeating the same sequence of rolls we had just finished, he called out, "Okay, that's enough! We're at our Bingo fuel—time to head back."

I would be lying if I said I wasn't smiling then. I righted the plane and transferred the control back to the pilot. He was silent for a moment, then said, "I guess I deserved that."

No comment.

Space walk training was one of the highlights of our ASCAN year. To prepare astronauts for the many space walks that were planned over the final years of the space station's construction, NASA was building a large underwater training facility. It would be another year before it was ready for training, though. In the interim, our space walk training took place in NASA's weightless environment training facility. The facility was basically a small pool on the main campus at the Johnson Space Center, one just big enough to fit the payload bay of the shuttle.

I quickly learned from the pool sessions that space walks were physically demanding. But as tiring as they were, the mental concentration was just as exhausting. As a space walker, you have to walk a fine line between overconfidence and hesitation. If you get too confident, you become arrogant, potentially making rash decisions. If you're too cautious, your indecision can be costly. Finding the balance is achieved through self-awareness. You have to be fully aware of every single thing you do. You can't let your focus waver even for an instant, because your or your partner's life may be at risk. Only when you're out of the airlock and your helmet is off can you finally start to relax. It was challenging, but the thrill and satisfaction of flawlessly executing a task after six hours in an underwater training simulator always made up for it.

Getting ready for the walks was much more involved and took far longer than any scuba diving I'd done before. I had a suit engineer, a suit technician, and often another astronaut helping me get into the suit, and even with all that assistance, getting dressed still took twenty to thirty minutes. The suit weighed around 280 pounds and had upper and lower torso parts joined by a waist seal. The upper torso mounted to a test stand. I'd pull on the lower torso and then stick my arms and head into the upper torso from below like a turtle trying to climb back into its shell. After connecting the cooling loop, the waist seal was secured and locked.

I loved being in the space suit underwater, and the more time I spent in it, the more confident I became that I could accomplish the various tasks. The suit gloves are cumbersome at first, kind of like wearing hockey gloves. It takes practice to use all the tools. At the end of a training session, my shoulders, back, and chest would be bruised

The underwater space walk exercises were some of the most challenging but most rewarding parts of my ASCAN training. *Photo courtesy of NASA*

and my fingernails often felt sore from all that work done in the gloves. Despite the physical challenges, I was excited whenever I got in the pool. I wanted to be considered for a spacewalking position on whatever mission I was assigned to, and to do that, I had to prove I was both competent and capable of performing all the necessary tasks.

So, needless to say, I was horrified when after my fourth training run in the pool I noticed a crack in the outer visor of my helmet. The suits we wore for training runs were old and the visors had an outer Plexiglas cover for protection. Somehow, during my run, that outer layer had cracked, and I had failed to notice.

How did that happen? I wondered. I thought back over every moment of the dive, but I couldn't recall when I might have hit something. *This isn't good.*

I caught the safety diver's eye, and he gave me a sympathetic smile as if to say, "To err is human." Although it was never spoken aloud that damaging equipment during a walk was an immediate disqualifier, I got the sense that, if I was going to be considered for a spacewalking assignment, I would have to step things up a notch and make no other errors.

After that training run, anytime I got into my space suit, I became hyperaware of my surroundings and how I was moving. *I will not be a bull in a china shop,* I thought.

The stress of having to constantly perform at my peak every day would have been much more taxing if it weren't for Cathy and Evan. Most nights—the ones when Cathy wasn't commuting to and from Toronto as a pilot, that is—I'd be home with both of them.

"How was your flight today?" she asked, knowing I'd done a flight to El Paso in the T-38.

"It was a 'too' flight," I said.

"A what?"

"A 'too' flight—too high, too low, too fast, too slow."

Cathy smiled. "Sounds like you're being a little hard on yourself."

I was now able to fly the airplane within 100 feet of the assigned altitude, but right on altitude at the right airspeed was where I should be and that was where I wanted to be. I knew the standard and I treated each flight as a chance to chase perfection.

It would have been easy to lose myself in manuals and checklists night after night or to worry about my progress. But the sound of Evan playing in his crib or splashing in the bath was always enough to bring me back to the real world.

I tracked my time in the NASA program according to Evan's growth. He was just an infant when we first moved to Houston. When I was learning to fly the T-38, Evan was starting to crawl and gurgle at us in his own baby language. By the time my graduation came around, he was trying to take his first steps.

My class graduated in just over a year. We were told this was quicker than any other NASA class before us. Graduation itself was a bigger deal than I had expected. A special evening was planned for us at the Gilruth Center at the Johnson Space Center, and our spouses and family members were invited. Everyone showed up to the ceremony in suits and dresses and with their families in tow.

When it was my turn to take the stage, I made my way to the front of the room, where Bob Cabana shook my hand with a quiet "Congratulations." Then, as he'd done for each of my classmates, he presented me with a silver pin. The first group of NASA astronauts—the Mercury Seven—had designed the pin. It featured a shooting star trailed by three curving streaks flying through a ring. Every astronaut got a silver pin after they graduated from NASA's training program, and a gold one when they returned from their first spaceflight.

I made my way off stage, back to Cathy and Evan.

"You did it!" Cathy said. "All those long days and late nights, and you made it."

"I couldn't have done it without you two," I said.

"So what's next?" Cathy asked.

I looked down at the pin in my hand. It was the culmination of years of intense training and study, and it promised the trip of a lifetime.

"Hopefully a flight assignment. We'll just have to see what the future brings," I said.

PART THREE

9

Mission STS-90, *Columbia*

Space is an immense, infinite void, full of grand and wondrous things. It's hard to know where to start when it comes to thinking about how we fit into it. The shuttles we fly on are intricate vehicles with approximately 2.5 million moving parts that represent the heights of human engineering and design. But despite how complex they are, they function only when the entire team works together and manages the smallest, simplest things. The perfect alignment of tiles on the undersurface of the orbiter. Picking up all tools and trash when work on the vehicle is complete. Such things might seem trivial, but only by focusing on every detail, by adhering to every protocol, and by committing to excellence every moment can you send humans to space and bring them back safely. The greatest accomplishments often have the most humble origins.

A few days after my graduation, I had just returned to my office after a workout at the astronaut gym and was shaking the rain off my jacket when my phone rang.

"Good morning, Dave." It was Bernadette Hajek, the assistant to Bob Cabana. "If you have a moment, Bob would like to speak with you."

"No trouble at all," I said. "I'll be right there."

I hung up and hurried out the door. Once again it felt as though I'd been called to the principal's office. Bob Cabana generally spoke to us one-on-one only when there was an issue with our training. And getting called to the boss's office without any explanation didn't exactly inspire confidence. *Why don't they ever tell us what these meetings are about?* I wondered as I took the stairs two at a time to my uncertain fate.

I knocked on his office door. "Dave, come on in," Bob said.

"Hi, Bob. What can I do for you?" I asked.

"Why don't you take a seat, Dave. I think you'll want to be sitting when you hear this news." Uh-oh.

I lowered myself into the chair opposite Bob. I waited. "Congratulations, Dave," he said. "You've been selected as a mission specialist for STS-90. You'll be flying on *Columbia*, on a sixteen-day shuttle mission. We're calling it Neurolab."

"Neurolab? As in neuroscience? In outer space?"

"It's the Decade of the Brain and NASA has committed a dedicated research mission to study how the brain and nervous system adapt to space. Your medical background will be invaluable, Dave."

It seemed too good to be true. Many astronauts waited months or years to be assigned to a mission that suited their skill set, so to find such a perfect fit so soon after finishing my ASCAN training was remarkable.

"I really can't believe it. Thank you so much, Bob," I said. "I'll bring everything I have to the mission."

"I know you will."

"Can I ask who I'll be flying with?"

"Rick Linnehan will be the payload commander, and two payload specialists will be chosen to fly with you from four that will train for the mission. The commander, pilot, and other mission specialist will be assigned later. In the meantime, you'll begin your mission training immediately."

I called Cathy as soon as I got back to my desk.

"Cathy, you'll never believe it. I've been assigned to a mission!" I said breathlessly.

"That's fabulous! When do you launch?"

"Not for another year at least, I imagine. It'll take a while to train for all the neuroscience experiments we'll be doing."

"Neuroscience—that's perfect for you! How long will you be up there?"

I paused. "Right now, it's scheduled to be a sixteen-day mission."

"Do you know what you'll be doing?"

"Not exactly. Not yet," I said. It dawned on me only then that although I had a general idea of what the mission entailed, I had no real idea of the specifics.

"Whatever it is, Dave, I'm sure it's going to be incredible," Cathy said.

It took several months for NASA to put together the rest of the crew, but finally, in early 1997, they were chosen. Our commander was Rick Searfoss, and I was thrilled to have two classmates with me, Scott Altman, our pilot, and Kathryn Hire, our flight engineer. We gathered in our crew office. They had just moved the contents of their desks to join us. It was time to get to know one another. The metal chairs squeaked as a couple of us leaned back and settled in for our introductions.

"Good morning, everyone. My name is Rick Searfoss, and I'm excited to be the commander for STS-90." Rick looked every bit the U.S. Air Force colonel that he was, lean and muscular with squared shoulders. "This is my third spaceflight and I'm looking forward to flying with you all."

Rick gestured to Scott. "Our pilot for this mission will be Scott Altman."

"Call me Scooter," said Scott as he leaned his six-foot-three frame back farther in his chair. "This is my first spaceflight, and I'm thrilled to be here."

"We'll have three mission specialists," Rick continued. He turned to Rick Linnehan across the table from me. "Rick—sorry, this is going to get confusing, isn't it?"

Rick Linnehan smiled. "Two Ricks on one shuttle. It'll be fun."

"I'm sure we'll figure it out," Rick S. said. "How was your last flight?"

"We had a great mission," Linnehan said. "I flew on STS-78 in '96. It was another life science mission, and Bob Thirsk was one of the payload specialists. Now we get to fly with Dave, and I'm already looking forward to another Canadian postflight tour."

"Rick will be in charge of all experiments during the mission, so any science questions go to him. Otherwise, come to me," our commander explained, before turning to Kay and me. "Dave and Kay, it looks like we'll have at least three rookie flying snails on board, but I understand there may be more."

"That's correct," Kay Hire said. Our class had changed its name from "the Slugs" to "the Flying Escargots" and one of Neurolab's experiments required us to bring more than a hundred snails on board with us.

"Don't worry. We'll make sure you and your friends get there and back in one piece," Rick S. said with a grin.

"Jay, Alex, Chiaki and Jim," Rick S. continued, "I understand two of you will be picked to fly with us in a few months. I'll let you know if I hear anything different." The payload specialists were scientists in their own right, technical experts who would operate various experiments during the mission. There was a talented group to choose from: Jay Buckey, an experienced space researcher, was an internist in the school of medicine at Dartmouth; Jim Pawelczyk was an expert in space cardio-vascular physiology and a professor at Penn State; Chiaki Mukai had already flown in space in 1994, was a cardiovascular surgeon, and had a PhD in physiology; and Alex Dunlap was a physician and veterinarian.

Rick continued. "All told, there will be seven of us on the shuttle when we take off, in addition to all the other creatures we'll bring with us."

"When will that be?" I asked.

"We're scheduled to fly in March 1998," Rick said. "There's just a couple of more things. Rick and Dave, I'd like you to be the contingency space walkers. We don't have any planned space walks for the mission, but if something breaks outside, you two will fix it."

This was great news. Perhaps the reports from my ASCAN space walk training were better than I thought.

"Also," he went on, "Dave will be one of the two crew medical officers. I'll choose the other after the payload specialist selection is made." *Doctors on the ground, doctors in space,* I thought. Months later, Jay and Jim were selected to fly the mission, and Rick chose Jay to be the second crew medical officer.

It was February 1997. My first thought was *Our trip is so far away!* But then I considered all the training and preparation we would need to do to become mission-ready, and suddenly a year didn't seem like much time at all. Cathy and I chatted about it later that night.

"It's hard to even think of everything that will happen between now and then," I said.

"So don't," Cathy said.

"What do you mean?"

"Just take it one step at a time. It's like the emergency department: you finish one case, and then you move on to the next."

I looked at Cathy admiringly. "Good point."

She got quiet then. "Dave, I have some news of my own."

I was expecting to hear that she was going to be switching to a different airplane, but when she announced, "We're going to have another baby!" I was thrilled. Meeting my new crew had been exciting, but it paled in comparison to the idea of meeting my newest child. Evan was now a very active young boy, and one of his favourite activities was to watch Disney's *The Lion King* while playing with his toys. Often we'd both fall asleep watching the exploits of Simba, me in my flight suit, tired from an afternoon in the T-38, and Evan in his pajamas on my chest. I couldn't wait until we added a younger brother or sister to the mix.

Cathy was still commuting back and forth to Toronto, and the next few months were a whirlwind. I spent my days learning how to become a proxy scientist for some of the best neuroscientists in the world, whose experiments we'd be conducting in space while they watched closely from the ground. At night I switched from reading books about the anatomy of baby mice to reading baby books to Evan as he drifted off to sleep. *Goodnight Moon* was his favorite.

In September 1997, I was about to enter a training session with Rick Linnehan, when one of the astronaut office assistants came running into the room.

"Dave," he said breathlessly. "Your wife called—it's time."

I looked up at Rick, but he was already waving me out of the room.

I jumped into the car and raced to the hospital to meet Cathy.

"How are you doing?" I asked breathlessly when I reached her room.

"I'm okay," Cathy answered, pausing to breathe slowly during a contraction. "I felt that one."

Several hours later we welcomed our new daughter, Olivia, into the world. Like Evan, Olivia was a quiet, good-natured baby. She seemed to have a permanent smile as she looked around the room at us—that is, until she got hungry. Then her cry let us know who was in charge.

Later that evening, while Cathy rested, I cradled Olivia in my arms. It struck me then how incredibly far away I was going to have to travel from my girl in just a few months' time.

"Don't worry," I whispered, holding her a little closer to my chest. "No matter how far away I go, you and your brother will always be right here."

Over the next few months, I tried to savor every single second I had at home. Evan was enjoying having a sister. Always attentive, he would bring her his favorite toy whenever she cried. When she was quiet, he was enthralled, but he didn't seem too impressed with her crying.

As our launch date crept closer, I grew increasingly cautious about our mission. Even something as simple as cutting an apple in the morning warranted extra attention: one slip of the knife would impact my ability to perform the complex dissections and surgery we would be doing in space. NASA had a list of prohibited activities within six months of launch, and while I was pretty sure I wouldn't be flying in any air races, the memory of being hit by a car on my bike as a child remained in the back of my mind. Anything can happen out of nowhere.

A couple of weeks before our launch, I was sitting at home in jeans and a T-shirt, reviewing the shuttle ascent checklist while eating dinner. I'd been spending more and more time at home, as I was about to enter the mandatory weeklong quarantine period that every astronaut goes through before a flight. I couldn't risk catching so much as a cold without risking being medically disqualified from the mission.

The house was quiet, and my checklist and notes were spread across our pine dinner table. Its worn surface had seen a lot over the years, each stain and chip a testament to the many predawn coffees and late-night celebratory meals we'd had together since medical school.

Suddenly the doorbell rang. I glanced up, irritated by the interruption. It rang again before I made it to the door. *We're not expecting anyone,* I thought. Through the door's stained glass panels, I could see a woman. She was moving anxiously from side to side, turning to look away and then looking back as if waiting for something of great importance. I opened the door and realized it was one of our neighbors from down the street.

"Do you know CPR?" she asked before I even said hello.

Please don't let this be a survey from the American Heart Association.

"Yes, I do know CPR. What can I do for you?" I replied.

"There's somebody down the street who's not breathing," she said.

My medical instincts kicked in and we ran down the street to her driveway, where a teenage girl was lying on the pavement. A couple of people were trying to do CPR, but it was obvious from a distance that things weren't going well. *They have no clue what they're doing,* I thought as I raced up to them.

"Let me in, please. I'm a doctor," I said.

The woman's pulse was faint and she wasn't breathing. Her skin was purplish from lack of oxygen. I knew immediately what to do, but I didn't have any of the resuscitation equipment I would typically use. I had a decision to make—fast. It was obvious this woman urgently needed to be ventilated, but without equipment, that meant giving her mouth-to-mouth. If I helped, I could save her life. But by doing so, there was a chance I could ruin my quarantine period and impact the mission.

The decision was easy. I started giving the woman mouth-to-mouth. *The flight surgeons are going to love this,* I thought.

As an emergency physician, I had resuscitated countless individuals from cardiac arrest but had always done so in the bright lights of a hospital room with advanced life support equipment, defibrillators, and a team of highly trained professionals. Even though I had spent years teaching lifesaving, this was the first time I'd given mouth-to-mouth in a real situation, far from a hospital. I was on my own, in a dark driveway, surrounded by distraught family members. Their anxiety was palpable, almost infectious, but when the first breath went in successfully and I felt the woman's lungs expand, I had hope.

As the air left the girl's mouth, I heard an obvious wheezing noise from her chest.

"Does she have asthma?" I asked the crowd behind me.

"Yes, but it's never been like this," the girl's mother said.

I continued giving breaths as the wail of the ambulance drifted from down the street. The paramedics arrived in a rush of noise and light.

"What happened?" the lead paramedic asked me.

"I believe she had a respiratory arrest following an asthma attack. She needs to be intubated and rehydrated, and we've got to give her bronchodilators." The paramedic looked at me in surprise. "I'm an emergency physician," I explained.

The two paramedics got right to work. They quickly realized that to save this girl we'd need the combined skills and efforts of all three of us. Within minutes we had reversed the course of the severe asthma attack. The girl was breathing on her own. The girl's mother and I both rode with the paramedics in the ambulance, and by the time we got to the hospital, the girl was conscious.

The next day I went into Johnson Space Center to see our flight surgeon, Dr. Smith Johnston. "Hey, how are things?" I said casually as I walked into his office.

"Great," he responded. "How are you doing? Ready for the flight?"

"Actually, there's something I need to tell you that may be relevant to the mission. I don't think it will be an issue, but just in case," I said, still trying to be as casual as possible.

"What's that?" Smith asked, leaning forward and looking me straight in the eye.

"Last night I had to perform mouth-to-mouth respiration on a teenager who had a respiratory arrest from status asthmaticus."

"You did *what*?" he asked looking at me in disbelief. I slowly repeated what I had said.

Smith leaned back in his chair, contemplating the full impact of what I'd told him. Finally he said, "Did she make it?"

"She did. The paramedics got there and I intubated her. We gave her fluids and some epinephrine, and she was starting to breathe by herself by the time we reached the hospital."

Then Smith got to the million-dollar question: "Did she have an upper respiratory tract infection? Pneumonia or anything else that caused the severe asthma attack?"

"Not that the family was aware of. They'd been painting inside the house and she had come over for a visit. Maybe that's what set off her attack," I said.

"Okay. Wow. How do you feel?"

"I'm fine. I'll let you know if I get any symptoms in the next couple of days, but overall I think the risk is low."

"I appreciate you telling me," Smith said. We continued to chat about some of the medical things that I might have to deal with as the crew medical officer. It didn't look like it would be a problem.

Our conversation came to a close. "Thanks again, Smith," I said. "I'll let you know if I don't feel well."

Just a couple of days before we were to go into official quarantine, the doorbell rang again. When I opened it, the girl and her parents were standing outside. She was bright-eyed and healthy.

"Can I come in?" she asked. "I wanted to talk to you about what happened earlier this week."

"Of course," I said, and we all went into the living room to sit down. Her parents shook my hand again, saying "Thank you" repeatedly. As we sat down in the living room, I thought about how unusual it was for me as a doctor to see someone after I'd cared for them. I had resuscitated lots of people in the hospital—sometimes successfully, sometimes not. But none of them had ever come by to say thank you, and I'd never spoken to any of them in a personal capacity afterward, especially not in my living room.

"I wanted to thank you," the girl said.

"Of course," I replied. "I'm a doctor—I was just doing my job."

"No, I don't think you understand," she said, her eyes burning into me. "I want to thank you for saving my life. I wasn't really sure what I wanted to do with my life. But after what happened, I'm thinking of becoming a doctor. It's incredible to think that, with the right skills, you can actually save a person."

I was stunned. In a few simple statements, she'd captured why I'd first wanted to become a doctor. These were the moments that made all the stress, studying, and challenges worthwhile. They call mouth-to-mouth resuscitation the "kiss of life." She was right: it's a rare gift to be able to save somebody's life. This girl's words were a reminder not to take that gift—or life itself—for granted.

"I'm really happy to hear you're interested in medicine. That's fantastic," I said. "I hope it works out for you." We parted ways and she went off with her parents' arms around her.

I returned my attention to the present. Thankfully, I didn't get sick, so there was nothing to worry about. The rest of the week was a blur, and before I knew it, quarantine and the launch were upon us.

We spent three days in quarantine in Houston before flying down to the Kennedy Space Center in our T-38s. After we arrived, Rick addressed a crowd of reporters and other onlookers, including our families.

"It's a beautiful day in Florida," he said. "From what I understand, *Columbia*'s doing great as we start the countdown. We're rested and ready to go."

When the questions finished, Cathy walked forward with Evan. I pulled a Woody *Toy Story* character out of my helmet bag to give him. He was thrilled. Olivia was with our nanny, Maria, back at the hotel, sleeping through the event.

The weather forecast looked good for the launch, and when we weren't reviewing our checklists or signing the stacks of photographs in the briefing room in crew quarters, we were at the beach. Since the early '60s, the astronauts had kept a beach house for use prior to

The NASA Beach House at Kennedy Space Center—here shown as it looked in the 1960s, before it was renovated—has been an important place for astronauts and their families for decades, giving us a place of peace to be before a flight. *Photo courtesy of NASA*

launch. It was part of a subdivision that NASA purchased to expand Kennedy Space Center, and it had become a special place for crew and their families prior to launch.

Forty-eight hours to go, I thought as I rolled onto my stomach to tan my back.

"Make sure you don't get sunburns on your backs," Rick yelled to us as we lay on the beach. "It can make it pretty painful lying in your seat for launch."

A little while later, there was a flurry of activity back at the beach house, and Rick called to us again. "We have to go back to crew quarters. The president wants to speak to us about the mission." We all leapt to our feet, grabbed our flip-flops, and ran to our convertibles. I had barely climbed into the back with Jay when Scooter took off, with Jim riding shotgun.

"You better slow down. We're still on the air force side of the Cape, and the MPs might give us a ticket," I yelled to Scooter.

"Not today they won't," he yelled back. "I have the perfect excuse: the commander in chief wants to talk to us."

Ten minutes later, we were in our blue flight suits in the crew quarters briefing room. Rick S., Scott, and Kay were seated at the table in front of us with Rick L., Jay, Jim, and me in a row behind them. We waited expectantly, looking at a video camera that would connect us to the president, who was touring the simulator building at JSC with Senator John Glenn and Peggy Wilhide, the head of public affairs at NASA headquarters. Peggy was excited about the Neurolab experiments and hoped we'd be able to brief the president on the research we would be doing.

"I hope you find out a lot of things about the nervous system," President Clinton said when he appeared on-screen, "because I'm getting to those years where I might need them."

"Thank you, Mr. President, we'll take that as one of the challenges we try to meet," commander Rick joked.

"What experiments will you be doing on Neurolab?" President Clinton asked. Clearly, Peggy had been able to capture the president's interest in the research.

Rick, Scooter, and Kay did their best to describe the science of the mission, but somehow they didn't quite capture it. When they got to the experiment on blood pressure regulation, Jim, who was the crew expert on it, looked as though he wanted to vault over them to answer it properly. After the interview, Peggy called, "Hey, great job, you guys, but you could have talked more about the experiments." I caught Jim's eye across the table and we both smiled.

The night before you lift off to go into space is tough. You're thinking about the mission and everything you will be doing, but you also find yourself wondering, *Is this my last night on Earth? What's going to happen? What if I don't come back?* Of course, you try not to dwell on those thoughts, but it's not easy. Most people don't get the world's best sleep the night before liftoff.

The day of the launch itself was scheduled down to the minute, with little time to spare. The last chance I had to talk with Cathy and the kids was the night before. I called their hotel. All the families were staying in nearby Cocoa Beach, ready to board buses that would bring them to the Cape to watch the launch the next morning.

"Evan, say good night to Dad," Cathy said, holding the phone to Evan's ear. But Evan was more interested in playing with Woody from *Toy Story* than he was in his dad's spaceflight.

"I'll see you soon, Evan," I said. "I love you."

Cathy took the phone back, and I caught Olivia cooing in the background. "Give Olivia a kiss for me," I said.

"I will," Cathy replied. "You better get some rest."

"I'll do my best."

"Try counting stars."

I had to laugh. "That might work."

"Be safe up there. I love you," she said.

"I'll be back before you know it," I said. "I love you, too."

I knew that Cathy was worried, and I admired her strength. She remained so calm and steady. The kids were too young to understand the risks, but Cathy knew as well as I did that the next day would be as dangerous as it was exhilarating.

10

The Longest Two Minutes of My Life

I awoke at 7:00 the next morning. Today I would be leaving the planet. Tonight, when I fell asleep, I would be in space. Breakfast was scheduled for 9:54, and we wouldn't get suited up to board *Columbia* until a couple of hours after that, so Jay, Jim, and I decided to go for a quick run. We had barely left crew quarters when one of the security vehicles slowed beside us.

"Haven't you heard?" one of the security guards called. "You guys have scrubbed for today."

"What happened?" Jay asked.

"One of the signal processors failed, and they have to change it out. The launch is rescheduled for tomorrow afternoon."

We turned around and ran back to crew quarters, where commander Rick confirmed the news. "They had a special meeting of the

mission management team and they're confident we'll launch tomorrow. The weather's good and there are no other issues with *Columbia*."

"Looks like we get another day at the beach house," Jay said.

I immediately called Cathy. "It's not a big deal," I said. "They just
need to change out one of the backup pieces of the comm system to be
sure that we can send experiment data to the ground if there's a failure
of the main system."

"Thanks for the update. I'm glad they decided early: gives me time
to take the kids to the beach."

"We're headed there, too. Have a great day. I'll call you tonight."

At 11:30, when we should have been boarding *Columbia*, we
climbed back into our convertibles and drove to the beach house for
lunch and a relaxing afternoon in the sun.

"So how do you feel?" Cathy asked in our call later that evening.

"I'm not thinking about it as much as last night. I feel ready, but
who knows. Something else might happen and we might scrub again
tomorrow," I said. "Say hi to everyone for me. Big hugs and kisses to
you and the kids."

The next day we were given the all clear, and we started our
prelaunch preparation at 10:15 a.m., right on schedule. We took the
crew photo and then headed to the suit room, where technicians helped
each of us into an orange advanced crew escape suit (ACES), which we
used for launch and reentry. When were were suited up, helmets in
hand, we stopped for an important ritual: watching Commander Rick
play a game of two-player poker with Bob Cabana. It was a tradition
dating back to the Mercury era; we couldn't leave until Rick lost. Fortunately, that didn't take too long.

We headed toward the elevator that would take us down to the
waiting crew transfer vehicle. We walked outside with Rick Searfoss in
the lead, Scooter behind him, and the rest of us following in line. We
were greeted by the cheers of hundreds of NASA team members who
had gathered to see us off. Climbing aboard the Astrovan, I looked at

the seats around me and imagined all those who had gone before me and those who would follow on their first trip to the launchpad. A lot had happened in the thirty-seven years since I first dreamt of becoming an astronaut. Who knows what might happen in the years to come?

"Third time's a charm, right, Rick?" Scooter asked, his moustache failing to conceal his grin.

"Every flight's a charm," Rick S. said. "And every flight's different, wouldn't you say, Rick?"

"Any spaceflight is a great spaceflight," Rick L. said.

"Kay, Dave, how are you doing?" Rick S. asked.

"I'm hoping it'll be easier to move in the suit once we're up there," Kay said.

"I couldn't agree more," I added. I'd spent hours in an ACES in training, but I still felt clumsy as I climbed down the steps off the van. It was hard to believe I'd be floating gracefully above the earth later that afternoon. Would it still be afternoon when we got to space?

We continued chatting and laughing with each other, and with the engineers and technicians, as we walked to the launchpad. Before we entered the elevator that would take us up 195 feet to the shuttle flight deck, I craned my neck to try to glimpse the top of *Columbia*, but I could barely see it at such a low angle. I stepped into the elevator, and when the doors closed behind us, it rumbled to life, starting the slow journey to the platform that would connect us to the shuttle. *I hope there's nothing in the countdown that causes us to scrub the flight,* I thought.

When we exited the elevator and stepped onto the platform, with the shuttle just a few steps away, the silence was all-encompassing. At 195 feet above the ground, we were higher than most birds fly, and I was struck by how peaceful everything was. The wind whistled lightly as it whipped past the elevator doors, and most of us moved to the handrail to stare out at the panoramic view and stand quietly in thought. The ocean waves rolled toward the shore, the sound of them lost in the distance. I glimpsed the launch control center across Banana Creek. *Cathy and the kids are there watching me.*

I thought back to other moments of stillness in my life. Sometimes they were restorative: sitting beside a gurgling stream in the woods behind my childhood home, or putting the kids to bed. Other times, such as the stunned silence in the emergency ward after I told a family I wasn't able to save their loved one, were more foreboding. *What will today bring?* I wondered.

The moment of reflection turned quickly to action as I was called to take my place on the flightdeck in the seat behind Scooter. The next two and a half hours flew by as we ran through our preflight checklists. I knew the checklist backward and forward: we'd run through it dozens if not hundreds of times, in simulators and in dry runs in the shuttle itself. If we missed any step or something wasn't done correctly, the consequences could be catastrophic.

"Check your tabs, close your visors, and turn your oxygen on," Rick called out. I glanced at my watch: two minutes until liftoff.

Some astronauts describe those two minutes as the longest in their lives. Others say they passed by in the blink of an eye. Which would it be for me?

The final step in my preflight list was to turn on the cockpit voice recorder. It was essentially a miniature cassette recorder that was mounted on the flight deck beside me. All I had to do was punch the "record" button.

I flicked the voice recorder on. Then there was a moment of stillness as though everything went on hold. Had time frozen? I glanced at the recorder and saw that the tape was rolling. Then, just for good measure, I checked it again. Everything looked nominal—astrospeak for "normal."

Finally, I lay back and looked forward out the windshield, which was really straight up to the sky. It was a crystal-clear blue day. The radio chatter slowed down, and once again, we were left with silence and our thoughts. My mind wandered back across the water to the spectator stands and the hundreds of guests, family, and friends who were there to witness our launch. It wasn't so long ago that I'd been on the outside looking in, just as they were now.

"T-minus thirty seconds," said the orbiter test conductor.

Reality was sinking in: this wasn't a simulation. Everything I'd done up to that point had been training. Now I was finally going to take the leap. *I'm about to go to space,* I thought. *I'm going to become a real astronaut.* I smiled at how simple the sentence was to say compared to how complex a process it had been.

"T-minus fifteen seconds."

In seconds I'd be hurtling toward my dream at twenty-five times the speed of sound, and eight minutes after that I would be 150 miles above the earth's surface. But if just a single thing went wrong, I might be thinking my last thoughts about Cathy, Evan, and Olivia. My skin broke out in a sweat, and I felt a sense of dread in my stomach. I was starkly confronted with my own mortality. I didn't have time to dwell on those fears, because at T-minus 6.6 seconds, the main engines ignited and I was back in astronaut flight mode.

"Three, two, one, zero. Liftoff, we have liftoff."

The solid rocket boosters ignited, and my world became nothing but noise. The first few seconds were violent. I felt the roar of the engines more than I heard it. I was shaking back and forth under the bone-rattling power of the solid rocket boosters. After two minutes of punishment, there was a massive *boom* and a bright orange light flashed outside the shuttle. For a moment I remember thinking we were about to blow up. Then my training kicked in. *It's just the solid rocket boosters separating, Dave,* the voice told me. I thought back to our training. "Solid rocket booster separation is pretty dramatic," Rick Searfoss had said with a grin. It was the understatement of a lifetime. The transition was like driving down a dirt road in the back of a pickup truck at 50 miles an hour, being bounced around, then suddenly going on a smooth ride on perfect, unblemished pavement. As we passed through the final layers of the earth's atmosphere, the view outside the window grew darker and darker.

The g-forces built to three times normal in the last minute before the main engine cutoff. It felt like an elephant was sitting on my chest. I fought to suck in a breath. My right arm slipped off my lap, and I was surprised by how difficult it was to lift it back into place. The main engine cut off, and the shuttle decelerated rapidly, throwing me forward against my harness. My body stopped, but my mind didn't. I felt like I was somersaulting uncontrollably head over heels. *It's just an illusion,* I told myself. I grabbed onto the seat and pulled myself firmly against it. The sensory cues from my body eventually reached my brain, breaking the illusion of tumbling.

When my mind finally caught up to my body, I got to work. I got out of my seat, folded it forward, and positioned myself on top of it to look out the overhead window. Kay was right there, eyes bright and wide. She passed me a Nikon camera with a large 400mm lens attached. I was about to start taking photos of the external tank when I noticed that the shutter speed and f stop that had been so carefully set before we took off had changed.

Glad I had a checklist to follow, I thought to myself. *Must have been knocked around by the vibrations during launch.* Every detail is critical for success.

Looking out the overhead window, I could see a silvery plume of excess propellant venting from the external tank. I was shooting with a film camera, so I had only thirty-six images available. I tried to time my shots perfectly, spacing them out to capture the tank from multiple angles as it fell away toward the earth. Beside me, Kay was video taping the same thing. The ground crew would use our work to inspect the external tank for areas of foam loss, the importance of which we'd only come to understand years later when *Columbia*, the same shuttle I was now flying on, disintegrated in the atmosphere above northeastern Texas during reentry.

For now, though, everything looked great. Kay and I gave each other a quick high five as we finished up, and I felt proud to have completed my first task of the mission. Rick and Scott were in their seats in front of us, with a number of tasks still ahead of them to position the shuttle into its orbital flight path. I stowed the camera away and then moved to the left side of the flight deck, where there was a little more room. I was almost giddy. For the first time outside of the simulated conditions of the Vomit Comet, I was experiencing true weightlessness. I looked out the overhead window, holding the back of Rick's seat as I admired the majestic view of our blue planet. "Spectacular," I said to myself. I took a deep breath, trying to savor the fact that my dreams had finally come true—I was in space!—and I let go of Rick's seat, my feet roughly six inches off the floor as I floated gracefully. With one finger I pushed the back of Rick's seat, hoping to turn and face aft for a better view of the earth.

Instead, I floated up and bumped into the window. Kay laughed. I tried to steady myself with my hands, but the next thing I knew, my feet were back down to the flight deck floor. I kept moving slowly back and forth between the floor and ceiling of the flight deck like a human Ping-Pong ball until I realized that I was pushing too hard with my hands and feet. After a bit of practice, I was finally able to float gracefully, moving with minimal effort despite the bulk of the launch-and-entry suit.

"Welcome to space," Rick said. "What do you think?"

"It's incredible," I said. "I see what you mean that only fingertip forces are needed to move around."

I went over to the ladder to head down to the mid-deck. In the simulator I had always gone down the ladder feetfirst. This time, though, I chose to go down headfirst, thinking to myself, *Why not? We're in space—might as well make the most of it.* A gentle pull with my right hand moved me slowly into mid-deck, where I floated by the ceiling as I looked down at Rick L., Jay, and Jim.

They were out of their seats and in the process of getting out of their suits. They'd undone the zippers on the backs of their suits and were trying to pull their heads and arms out of the upper bodies of their suits. Jim was holding Jay, who seemed to be going through a series of contortions while trying to extricate his head and arms. I floated over to help Rick, then Jim and I recruited their help to get us out of ours.

Our next job was to change *Columbia* from its launch configuration to its orbit configuration. We used every available nook and cranny to stow away the launch equipment and create the space needed to turn our shuttle into a living laboratory.

In many ways it reminded me of cleaning up your apartment when your parents are coming over for dinner. Clothes that haven't seen a hanger in months are pushed under the bed, stacks of books and papers are shoved under the sofa, dishes are loaded in the dishwasher. Except, instead of clothes, books, and dishes, we were rolling up our ACES suits, removing and folding the mid-deck seats, and trying to find places for our floating helmets and gloves. In the absence of gravity, things don't stay where you put them unless they're tethered, Velcroed, or stuck under a bungee cord. After an hour and a half, we had everything set up and were able to settle in for our first evening in space.

"Sorry, Rick, I almost kicked you," I said as I floated over to the galley. I was still getting used to the fact that there was no up or down anymore. I watched Rick grab a meal package from a cupboard, push himself backward, spin around, and grab the wall on the other side. He was pretty good at this!

"How long does it take to become accustomed to this whole weightless thing?" Kay asked as she floated down from the flight deck.

"Might take a day or so," Rick said as he opened his meal and passed Kay hers.

"It's still a little strange getting used to hanging out on the ceiling," I said.

"Just wait until you brush your teeth," Rick said.

We had selected all of our menu and food choices months before in a lengthy food-tasting session. As I opened the mid-deck food locker, I thought, *What on earth possessed me to choose beefsteak and shrimp cocktail for my first meal in space?* I added water to some granola and ate some almonds and a tortilla while the granola hydrated.

There are two critical tools for eating in space: scissors and a spoon. We had knives and forks available, but we'd been told it was easier to cut food packages open and eat with just a spoon rather than trying to juggle floating sharp and pointy cutlery. I watched a piece of rice float out of Scooter's meal bag, and he didn't even bother with the spoon; he just snapped it out of the air. With seven of us now on the mid-deck, some trying to get our food from stowage lockers and others changing into crew shirts and pants, it was pretty crowded. There is no test of teamwork quite like eating your dinner when someone floats by trying to pull their pants on. After lots of laughs at our clumsiness and more than one attempt to catch free-floating food, we finally finished dinner and started to get ready for bed. It had been a long day.

As we lined up to use the toilet, the two veteran Ricks watched with amusement as the rest of us tried to get over the varying degrees of motion sickness we were having. Unlike long airplane flights where your feet get bigger and it is hard to put your shoes back on, in space your face gets puffy and your legs become very thin as fluid shifts from your lower limbs to your upper body and head.

"So this would be the puffy-face, bird-leg syndrome you talked about?" I asked.

"That's it," Rick Searfoss said with a laugh. "Looks great on you."

"Thanks," I said. "I feel stuffed up; it's like having a cold." As the crew medical officer, I was responsible for everyone's health, so I doled out medication to ease people's stomachs before heading to my sleep station to get ready for bed.

I grabbed my toothbrush and toothpaste from my personal hygiene kit, which I had temporarily Velcroed to the wall. *Does anything in space not have Velcro attached to it?* I thought. I used the galley to squirt a blob of water onto my toothbrush. When I talk to kids in schools, they often ask how the water stays on the toothbrush in outer space. "Surface tension," is always my answer. I explain how the beads of water cling to the toothbrush's surface and prevent it from floating away.

Halfway through brushing, it struck me that we didn't have a sink on the shuttle.

"What do you do with the toothpaste?" I asked Rick Searfoss.

He chuckled. "Spit it onto the corner of your facecloth. Just make sure you wash your face first."

Marvelous, I thought as I grabbed my facecloth.

"And, Dave," Rick said with a serious tone. I spun around, wondering what I'd done wrong. "Just make sure you grab your *own* facecloth. I don't want to end up washing my face with your backwash."

"Don't worry, I've got mine," I responded before taking a close second look that I had the correct one.

Finally, I made my way back to my sleep station. On most shuttle flights, the commander and pilot put their sleep restraint systems—basically, sleeping bags—on the flight deck while the rest of the crew finds a place to sleep in the mid-deck. But four of us—Jay, Jim, Rick L., and I—were subjects in a sleep study experiment, so we'd each been given a small sleep station, roughly the size of a broom closet. Each one had a sliding door to seal us in, giving us a bit more privacy than most people had when sleeping in space.

We all said good night and I slid my door closed. I quickly went through my crew notebook in preparation for the next day, and then I switched off the reading light and closed my eyes. I'm one of those people who doesn't like to be too warm when they sleep, so I chose to lie on top of my sleeping bag rather than in it. I thought about how often Cathy told me that I tossed and turned in my sleep, alternating between stealing the covers or throwing them aside. *No worries of that tonight,* I realized as I drifted off.

I woke up to the song of the day being played by Mission Control.

Our CapComs promised us a different "brain-related" song every morning, and as I peeled open my eyes, Aretha Franklin's "Think" filled the mid-deck. *What a fantastic sleep!* I thought. I felt energized for my first full day in space. Still marveling at how incredible it was to be there, I reached over my left shoulder to slide the door open. But the door handle and the door were gone.

Great: my first night in space and I'm stuck in my sleep station. I searched again, thinking that perhaps I'd just missed seeing the handle that would cue me as to the whereabouts of the door. But no. It was gone. I knew the reading light was right above my head, so I reached up to turn it on and orient myself, only to find the light wasn't there, either. I debated knocking on a random wall of my sleep station and calling for one of my crewmates to let me out, but my pride wouldn't let me. Instead, I rolled ninety degrees to my right and tried to locate the door by my left shoulder. After a couple of tries, I found it. I slid it open.

"Good morning," I said to the crew, who were staring at my sleep station from the galley.

Jim looked over at me as he sipped his coffee from a straw connected to one of the Kona coffee drink bags. "What exactly were you doing in there?" he asked. "It sounded like you were flailing around."

"Nope, just stretching," I responded with a smile as I floated out of the sleep station and over to the bathroom—otherwise known as the waste containment system. *No more falling asleep on top of the sleeping bag,* I thought.

I wolfed down a quick breakfast and headed to the lab. We might still be adjusting to life in space, but we had a busy schedule. The day was packed with experiments down to the minute.

Space was a perfect place to study brain adaptation. We had twenty-six experiments scheduled for our mission: fifteen that involved research animals, and eleven in which we were the test subjects. The experiments in which the crew were the subjects examined changes in our blood pressure, balance, orientation, motor performance, and

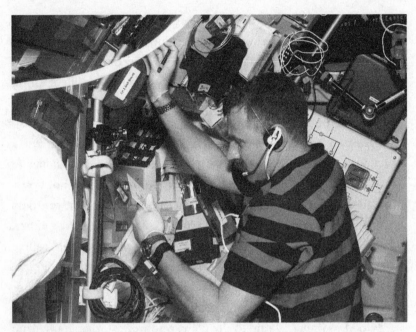

Most of our days during the mission were spent either performing experiments on the shuttle or serving as subjects for them. *Photo courtesy of NASA*

sleep. The animal experiments used the absence of gravity to study how the brain and nervous system would adapt and whether walking behavior learned in space would be forever different or would revert to normal when the animals returned to Earth.

When I trained as a neuroscientist, many thought that the brain was hardwired, as though the neurons in the brain were static, like the connections on the motherboard of a computer. Much of the Neurolab research was investigating a new idea called neuronal plasticity. It was a theory that brain connections could change and adapt over time. It would be somewhat like a computer that can rewire itself to improve its speed and function. If we could understand how the brain modified and created new connections, we might be able to use that knowledge to help patients recover from strokes or brain injuries.

Many of the tests we ran involved detailed, precise surgery on rats to help understand the exact changes taking place in the nervous system as they adjusted to space. The surgery and dissections required precision, focus, and dexterity, so when I was in the middle of a task, it was easy to lose track of time; hours could pass by in what felt like an instant. Often lunch had come and gone before I was able to finish.

"How's it going, Dave?" Rick Linnehan asked as he passed by.

"Right in the thick of things," I said. "You have a protein bar on you?" After four hours, I was ready for a break.

Rick tossed me a protein bar, the wrapper glinting in the overhead light as it spun lazily toward me.

"Is that going to be enough?" he asked.

"It's just like being back in med school," I said, cramming the food into my mouth. "Work, eat, sleep, repeat."

We had a miniature zoo on board the flight with us. We were flying with adult and newborn rats, mice, crickets, oyster toadfish, swordtail fish—a whole menagerie of fins, legs, and tails. The animals were key to our Neurolab experiments, and it was critical to keep them healthy. Partway through the mission we checked on the animals and found that some of the newborn rats were dehydrated. The mothers weren't nursing them properly. Small wonder: the trip had been intense enough for us humans, so I could only wonder what it had been like for these little creatures. Jay, Jim, and I got together with our onboard veterinarian, Rick Linnehan, to discuss the situation.

"We need to get water into them," Rick said.

"How?" I asked. "It's a bit of a challenge starting an IV on a baby rat."

"We'll just have to try it a different way," Rick said.

So, under Rick's direction, Jay and I became impromptu vets. We gathered syringes, filled them with water, and fed some of the rats by hand. If they were really dehydrated, we also injected small amounts of sterile water beneath their skin. As a physician I knew that this technique, called hypodermoclysis, can be used in human patients if necessary, so it wasn't a surprise when Rick suggested it for the rats.

"Did you ever think you'd be running a rat ICU in space?" I asked Rick.

"It wasn't the first thing that came to mind when I trained to be a vet," he replied as he applied some antibiotic cream to a scratch on a newborn rat.

Thankfully, we were able to save most of the animals, and with daily supplemental hydration, the experiments could continue as planned. The rats lived in animal enclosure modules and we brought them in their special cages to the glove box, a large glass enclosure with two arm sleeves built into it that allowed us to do the experiments. I watched as one rat climbed up the sleeve of my left arm, now inside the box, and kicked off with its hind legs. It floated over to my right sleeve, where it latched on with its front paws and pulled itself onto my arm. It ran down that arm and then leapt back to my left glove, its whiskers twitching as it glided across the cage. I considered what I was seeing: a rat in outer space that had learned (maybe even faster than I had) how to adjust to zero gravity. It was incredible. And it wasn't just that rat: the others would do it, too.

They're playing, I thought as I smiled to myself. *They've learned how to float!*

NASA had carefully built our schedules for us, and they included PSA—pre-sleep and post-sleep activities, our downtime. They wanted to make sure we had time to recharge our batteries and get our rest. But we found we often cut into our rest time to set up or finish our experiments. Even our rest itself was an experiment, as our sleep cycles were being measured each night.

"How was your PSA last night?" I asked Jay blearily one morning as we gathered for breakfast. We had been up late caring for the rats.

"You mean my post-science activity?" he asked. "About the same as my pre-science activity this morning: trying to catch up or get ahead."

There were a number of cameras on board, and the research team back on Earth was hoping we'd be able to take lots of pictures of the experiments. Over the course of the mission, we got some great photos of the science, but often we didn't have the time to take pictures and stick to the timeline. We were working sixteen-hour days just trying to prepare for and get through everything on the schedule. I didn't mind it a bit, though. The hopes and dreams of a team of international scientists were riding on us. Every little piece of knowledge we brought back with us had the potential to change our understanding of the nervous system.

By the time we had an afternoon off, it was halfway through the mission. I had been looking forward to it all week. Our email and video call capabilities weren't that great on the shuttle, so any conversations with our families were carefully choreographed. But I had something up my sleeve.

During the mission Cathy was still working full-time, and that particular day she was the first officer on a flight from Toronto to Montréal. The plane was halfway to its destination when Cathy noticed the datalink starting to print.

The captain glanced at Cathy, then turned back to the datalink. "It looks like this is for you," he said. "I think it's from the space shuttle."

"That's incredible," Cathy said. "Pass it over."

She read the first line aloud, "We are having a great time orbiting the earth at mach 25 much higher than the flight levels."

"Give me that," the captain said with a grin before flicking on the plane's PA system. "Ladies and gentleman, this is the captain. We just received a special message that I'd like to share with you." He proceeded to read the note over the PA system to the passengers. The entire plane burst into applause when he finished.

Later in the mission I would have a chance to chat with Cathy while she was on a layover in Los Angeles.

"Hi there," I said, my voice faint and crackling over the line. "We're over Australia right now."

```
FLIGHT AC0432/24    YYZ-YUL    FIN-215
TIME 12:16:32              DATE 98.04.24
------------------------------------------------
-// PNT P026 YYZWGAC 24APR/1215 YYZ1      C-FTJQ/
CATH..
WE ARE HAVING A GREAT TIME ORBITING THE EARTH
AT MACH 25 MUCH HIGHER THAN THE FLIGHT LEVELS.
PLEASE EXTEND THE BEST WISHES OF THE CREW OF
STS-90 COLUMBIA TO THE CAPTAIN, THE CREW AND
ALL OF THE PASSENGERS. MAY EVERYONE ENJOY THEIR
DESTINATION AS MUCH AS WE ARE ENJOYING SPACE.
TAKE CARE.
LOVE DAVE
FROM THE FLIGHT DECK OF STS-90
```

Sending a message from the space shuttle to Cathy's cockpit was one of the highlights of my mission.

"Unbelievable," Cathy said. "It's great to hear your voice. How are things going?"

"We've been working nonstop, but everything's been going smoothly. How are Evan and Olivia?"

"They're great. Olivia is crawling everywhere—she's really motoring along."

"Probably trying to keep up with her big brother. I miss you all."

"We miss you, too. I'm glad things are going well, and we'll see you before long."

When it was time to finish the call, I looked out the flight deck overhead window to see where we were. Excitedly I said, "We're just coming up to the coast of California. I can see the lights of San Diego below us and Los Angeles in the distance."

"From Australia to LA in one phone call. Wow!" Cathy said. "Have fun, be safe, and we're all looking forward to having you back on the ground. Love you."

I was saying "Love you, too" when Mission Control interrupted: "That's all the time you have, Dave."

My mother, Isobel, was an operating room nurse. She loved her work and shared her passion for medicine with my sister and me.

My dad, Bill. If I got the exploration gene from anybody, it was him. He had a fascination with aviation and a passion for human spaceflight.

My friend Bryan and I at the two-storey fort we built in 1964. We weren't too concerned about trimming the discarded lumber we found.

As a kid, I had a fascination with vehicles of all kinds—space shuttles, planes, cars, and, yes, even trains.

Hiking through the brush at Camp Kanawana in 1963.

At twelve, I decided I wanted to learn to dive. I was really young to start lessons, so my dad had to negotiate with the instructor on my behalf just to get me into class. I learned to skin dive first and then finished my scuba training.

All suited up for a dive in Maine in 1968.

I loved cruising around on my motorcycle, and I never left home without my helmet and gloves. Being hit by a car as a young boy taught me that safety always comes first.

One of the first planes I learned to fly was this, a Cessna 150.

One of the highlights of our training with
the Canadian Space Agency was flying in
the KC-135, or what we affectionately called
the Vomit Comet. *Photo courtesy of NASA*

On the KC-135. The only way to simulate a zero-gravity environment was to fly endless parabolas on the Vomit Comet to get used to using tools while floating weightless. *Photos courtesy of NASA*

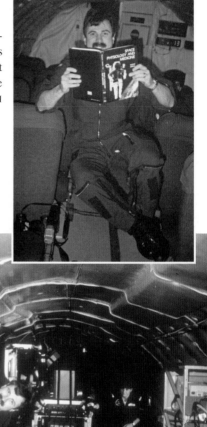

They say that when you do what you love, you'll never work a day in your life. That adage definitely applied to my training days—I'd never had so much fun. *Photo courtesy of NASA*

Our cold-weather survival training taught me just how close I could get to a fire without singeing my clothes. *Photo courtesy of NASA*

Some of the Flying Escargots, also known as the ASCAN class of 1994, experiencing weightlessness on the KC-135. I'm in the top row, third from the left. *Photo courtesy of NASA*

I'll never forget my excitement the first time I went supersonic in one of the NASA T-38 jets. It was everything I had imagined as a kid when I read *The Right Stuff*. *Photo courtesy of NASA*

In 1996, I was selected as a mission specialist for STS-90, flying on *Columbia*, on a sixteen-day shuttle mission. It was called Neurolab. *Photo courtesy of NASA*

The sight of the shuttle *Columbia* ready to lift off was equal parts terrifying and inspiring. *Photo courtesy of NASA*

On STS-90, my first spaceflight, I learned that there is no such thing as up or down in space. Top (left to right): Kathryn Hire, Jay Buckey, James Pawelczyk, and me. Bottom (left to right): Scott Altman, Richard Searfoss, and Richard Linnehan. *Photo courtesy of NASA*

On Neurolab, we were both scientists and test subjects. On this particular day, Jim Pawelczyk performed a ball-catch experiment testing his sensory motor skills while I worked on another experiment in the glove box. *Photo courtesy of NASA*

Me (far right) diving with my crew outside of Aquarius, an underwater research station located off the coast of Key Largo, Florida. The NASA Extreme Environment Mission Operations (NEEMO) sends groups of astronauts, engineers, and scientists to live and train in Aquarius, which simulates conditions on the International Space Station. *Photo courtesy of NASA*

From Aquarius, we'd dive along one of the excursion lines—ropes suspended above the bottom of the ocean floor that led from the habitat to various parts of the reef. Getting lost would be catastrophic, so we followed the ropes with the same rigor we would use our tethers in a space walk. *Photo courtesy of NASA*

Much of our training for missions involved virtual reality and simulators that helped us train the way we would fly so that, eventually, we would fly the way we trained. *Photo courtesy of NASA*

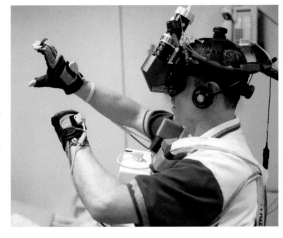

Cathy and I have two amazing children. Our son, Evan, was born in 1994, and our daughter, Olivia, in 1997. We took this picture just before I left on STS-118. *Photo courtesy of NASA*

Floating with my STS-118 crewmates. Back (left to right): Charlie Hobaugh, Tracy Caldwell, Rick Mastracchio, and me. Front (left to right): Alvin Drew, Barbara Morgan, and Scott Kelly. *Photo courtesy of NASA*

No matter how far away I flew, my family was always with me. *Photo courtesy of NASA*

In my spacesuit ready for a space walk. I completed three during my second space-flight on STS-118, setting a Canadian record in the process. *Photo courtesy of NASA*

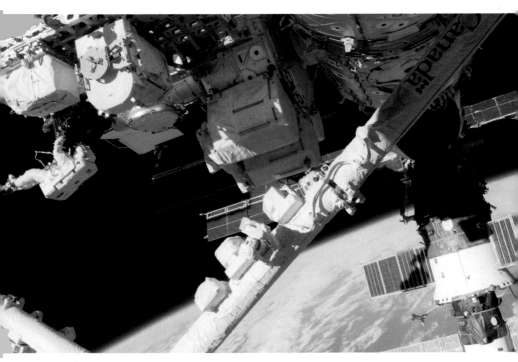

Riding the Canadarm II during my second space walk on the International Space Station. It's one thing to be inside a spacecraft looking out the window at the Earth, but it's something else entirely when you put on a spacesuit and step "outside." *Photo courtesy of NASA*

Hard at work during my STS-118 space walks. My training in the pools in NASA had taught me well—after my three space walks, there wasn't a scratch to be found on my visor. *Photos courtesy of NASA*

Here I am in my role as "Dr. Dave" at Sunnybrook Health Sciences. One of the great parts about working on the trauma team at the hospital was that everyone brought their best to the trauma room. It was always easier to chart a path forward and solve a problem when you weren't doing it alone. *CSA*

Cathy remains a proud member of the Ninety-Nines, the international organization of women pilots.

The views of our blue planet from the end of the Canadarm II were the most spectacular sights of my life. *Photos courtesy of NASA*

The next day we were back in the lab doing a rotating chair experiment to test the adaptation of our inner ear to space. After we completed the experiment, it was time for dinner, but when we got to the mid-deck we were surprised to see Rick L., Scooter, and Kay working on something under the floor panels.

"What's going on?" I asked.

"I heard a strange noise beneath the mid-deck floor, and then we got an alarm," Kay said. "It looks like the carbon dioxide scrubber has shut down."

"Everything's fine now," Rick added. "Mission Control asked us to switch to the second set of control electronics and restart it. But about ten minutes later it shut down again. We've just installed backup carbon dioxide absorption canisters for now until the ground team figures out a better solution."

We were more worried about the mission being shortened than we were about any crew risk associated with the system not working properly. We knew the ground team would take care of us, but I was concerned about what information would be passed along to Cathy. I didn't want her reading about this in the newspaper. Neither did Mike Bloomfield, one of our NASA family escorts. Mike was one of my classmates and was there to support our families if something happened during the mission, in addition to the support provided by the CSA, and he called Cathy to give her an update.

The next morning we woke to the sound of "Every Breath You Take" by the Police, a great choice by our CapCom that day in light of the problems we were having with the CO_2 system. The engineers had found the source of the issue: a leaky valve.

"It must be Saturday—time to work on our car, just like down on Earth," Rick S. joked with Mission Control. With the advice of experts on the ground, he was able to solve the problem simply by loosening a clamp, disconnecting a hose, and placing some aluminum tape over the leak.

"Everything is working as expected," Mission Control radioed after the system was powered back up. "Looks like we won't need to shorten the mission."

"That's great news," Rick said. "Thanks for working all night to get the answer for us."

Rick and Scooter went up to the flight deck to practice landings on a laptop computer simulator, and I got ready for an interview with BBC Wales. Proud of my heritage and as a tribute to my father, I had brought some Welsh memorabilia with me, including the rugby cap of the famed Sir Gareth Edwards. I finished the interview by speaking Welsh—definitely a first—and despite my poor accent my message apparently touched many.

On one of our final mornings in space, I was scheduled for some exercise, so I went up to the flight deck, where we'd installed a stationary bike. I buckled myself onto the seat and started cranking the pedals. As I looked out the window, Mount Everest came into view, its peak rising above the mountains around it. After a few minutes the mountains gradually disappeared, replaced by the roads and cities of eastern China. As we passed over North America, I admired the beauty of the Rockies as the sun set behind us. It seemed surreal watching the earth through the overhead windows as I cycled on the exercise bike. There were no lines demarcating countries, making it clear that, despite different cultures and languages, we are all in this together. We are all inhabitants of Spaceship Earth.

A little over an hour later, my exercise time was up, and I slowed my pedaling. I took one last look out the window and saw that the Himalayas were just coming into view again.

Look at that, I thought. *I just biked around the world in an hour and a half.*

As our sixteen days came to a close, I knew I would miss the experience when I got back home. As much as I desperately wanted to be with Cathy and the kids again, I also knew it was possible that I might not get a second opportunity to live in space. Of course, I wanted to fly on another mission, but I couldn't predict what might happen.

"Do you miss it when you get back home?" I asked Rick Searfoss at one of our last meals.

He paused. "It's like any long trip," he said. "You might have had incredible experiences, but you've planned for it to be a certain amount of time. When it's time to go home, it's time. You miss it when you return home, but you're still glad to be back."

When it came time for reentry, we checked that the animals were doing well in their enclosures, stowed all the equipment in the Spacelab, and spent half a day cleaning the lab. The stationary bike on the flight deck was put away, and the seats we strapped ourselves into during liftoff came back out. We were all drinking water and electrolytes constantly as we pulled on our suits and hooked up the coolant systems. The last thing we wanted was to overheat and faint on the way back.

The night before landing, we had a final crew dinner together. It was a fantastic celebration and we ate whatever we wanted, no longer worried about having enough food for the remainder of the mission. The brownies and M&M's all disappeared.

"We're coming to the end of an incredible mission," Rick S. said. "Thanks for being such a fantastic crew. The teamwork was incredible. From my perspective that's why we were able to fix the CO_2 scrubber, take care of the sick rats, and succeed with all the experiments. Perhaps the data will change the way we understand the nervous system. Great work. It's been an honor flying with all of you."

Soon, we would be back on Earth and we'd each be pulled in different directions, but for those precious moments we were content to share our success together, just the seven of us floating freely in space.

Rick Linnehan and I swapped seats for the reentry, so I wasn't on the flight deck. Instead of Scooter right in front of me, I had a wall of mid-deck lockers. Unlike the many instruments on the flight deck that we all monitored as a team, I now had only the cabin altimeter—the device that measured the pressure inside the shuttle—to look at. The good news was it held steady. As we entered Earth's atmosphere, I managed to get a brief glimpse outside through the window on the side hatch. All I could see was an orange blur flickering around the shuttle, a blur that grew with every passing second. Beyond that, there was nothing but a deep, all-encompassing blackness.

After helping Jay and Jim get strapped in, I floated over to my seat. I pulled my parachute on and settled in, reaching around for the straps of my five-point harness. When I was finally secured, I plugged in my oxygen line and communications cord, fastened my helmet, and pulled on my gloves.

I turned my attention back to the checklist floating in front of me. I could hear the other crew members over the radio. Scooter and Rick Searfoss did most of the talking, keeping us and the Mission Control team updated on where we were. As our altitude dropped, I could feel the effects of gravity coming on. My arms began to feel heavier, and my helmet felt like it weighed more. My body was pushed into the seat, making it more and more difficult to look over at Jay and Jim beside me. Gradually the checklist that had been floating in front of me moved toward the floor and hung limply from its restraint. We were now feeling the full effects of gravity. The shuttle gave a slight shudder, almost like a car going over railroad tracks, as we broke the sound barrier and became subsonic. We were back.

Rick guided the shuttle around a partial circle and then rolled out to line up with runway 33 at Kennedy Space Center. A few minutes later *Columbia* rolled to a stop after traveling continuously at twenty-five times the speed of sound for the past sixteen days.

"Congratulations, everyone, welcome back to Earth," Rick S. called over the intercom.

The flight deck crew continued the post-landing checklist, but for us it was time to relax. "I'm going off comm now," I said.

I undid my five-point harness, popped off my helmet, and pulled it off my head. Turning my head to find my helmet bag took incredible effort, as though my head weighed ten times as much as normal. I slowly placed my helmet into its bag and lowered it to the floor.

"Who put bricks in my helmet bag?" Jim called out.

"I feel like I'm carrying a couple of weights from the gym," I said.

I looked over at Jay and Jim. They both flashed a thumbs-up. The three of us remained seated in mid-deck, waiting for the crew transfer vehicle and a couple of stretchers. There was nothing wrong with us, but we were on strict orders to avoid standing up. We were all part of an experiment to understand the control of blood pressure in space and on landing. After the ground crew opened the doors, they carried us off the shuttle horizontally, while the rest of the crew walked upright behind us.

I'd been looking forward to seeing trees, water, and the scenery of the cape on the way back to crew quarters. Instead, I found myself staring up at the ceiling of the crew transfer vehicle as we rolled off the runway. Once we were back in crew quarters, the technicians wheeled the three of us to tables with straps to hold us in place. The tilt tables were used to test how our blood pressure and heart rate would respond to gravity when we were tilted from lying flat to standing vertical. I had not felt light-headed during the flight back, but after a few minutes in a standing position my vision started to blur. Just when I thought I was about to pass out, the team lay me flat on my back once more.

"All right, Dave. You're free to get up," said one of the researchers. It felt like I'd been in bed for weeks, almost as though I were stuck in place. I stood up gingerly and everyone eyed me suspiciously. Perhaps I wasn't looking my best. Maybe I was a little pale as blood shifted back to my legs. "Is there anything we can get you?" one of them asked.

"A cheeseburger and a chocolate shake would be great," I said.

"No problem."

I was half joking about the burger, but as soon as we finished the data collection, a huge burger, golden fries, and a thick chocolate shake were waiting for me. After eating freeze-dried space food for two weeks in space, the cheeseburger was just what the doctor ordered. Few things have ever tasted so good.

As I was wiping the last of the cheese off my chin, the doors to the quarters opened, and Cathy and the kids came hurtling in. I stood up and folded my wife into a big hug.

"I'm so happy to see you," I said.

"We're so glad you're back," Cathy replied. I bent down to scoop Evan into my arms as he tried to snag one of the fries.

"I missed you, Evan," I said. He smiled at me, then turned his attention back to the fries. I bent down to Olivia's stroller to give her a kiss. She was asleep, and her feet wriggled lightly as my stubble brushed her cheek.

"I want to hear all about it," Cathy said. "But we've been waiting here for a couple of hours, and Evan is getting antsy—and hungry, as you can see."

"Why don't you head back to the hotel," I suggested. "We need to go through a few more debriefings anyway. No point staying here when you can be on the beach."

A few hours later I was finally finished and allowed to properly reunite with Cathy, Evan and Olivia. We would be heading back to Houston the next day and we spent the last of the afternoon and evening soaking up the sun by the hotel pool. I savored the breeze in my face and the smell of the lush vegetation by the pool. My skin greedily absorbed the warm rays.

I spent hours telling Cathy about every little thing I could remember from the mission. In between my "And thens" and "Did I tell yous," she filled me in about what Evan and Olivia had been doing in the weeks I'd been away.

That night, after Cathy and I had put the kids to sleep and turned off the lights, I lay in the hotel bed looking up at the ceiling. My mind was still trying to sort through everything: I half expected to start floating toward the ceiling, but my limbs were firmly glued to the sheets. I ran my hands over the bedspread, thinking, *Sure beats having to Velcro myself into bed.*

"Was there any single moment that stood out to you?" Cathy whispered as we were dozing off.

My mind spun through a series of images: floating around while eating dinner with my crewmates, watching a rat learn to navigate zero-g, the Himalayas stretching out beneath the window.

"It's hard to pick just one. Everything was remarkable, but I think I liked the sunrises the most," I said.

"Do you think life back on Earth can ever compare?" Cathy teased.

I thought about our kids, asleep in the room beside us. They were such little things then, but who knew what great things lay ahead of them? "I wouldn't trade this for anything else."

11

The Other Frontier

What did it take for the first human to walk on the moon? Incredible feats of engineering, immense resources, and remarkable courage on the part of everyone involved. But there is one thing that was needed above all else: imagination. Throughout history, space had been the subject of countless myths, stories, and fantasies. Sending a human being to the moon, let alone space, seemed impossible. But impossibility is just opportunity waiting to happen. Where once the skies seemed like the limit for humanity, now we can travel freely beyond them. With the right mind-set and combination of skills, anything is possible.

While we were in space, we heard that there was interest in a second Neurolab mission. There were delays in the International Space

Station program that had opened a three-month gap in the shuttle flight schedule. It was unheard-of for a crew to go from one mission to another immediately after landing; needless to say, we were pretty excited. Unfortunately, a few days after we returned, NASA decided that they wouldn't go ahead with the follow-up mission. Our crew became part of the regular astronaut pool.

So, in late June 1998, I was back in the STS-90 crew office signing photos and going through a backlog of emails. It had been a whirlwind of debriefs, tours, and travel from Houston to Canada, but things were finally settling down a bit. I received another call from Bernie, Bob Cabana's assistant.

"Dave, Bob wants to see you again."

By now I was getting better at not reacting when the corner office called. "I'm free this afternoon. Will that work?" I said.

There was a pause and then Bernie said, "Sure. Come by at 1400."

"Okay, I'll see you then."

Bob was sitting behind his desk when I arrived. "How have you been adjusting to life back on Earth, Dave?"

"Pretty well, all things considered. Showers feel like a luxury."

"I'm sure they do." Bob cut to the chase. "I wanted to talk to you about your collateral duty assignment. You've been assigned as a capsule communicator, and we want you to start your training as soon as possible. With all the crews being assigned to ISS construction flights, we need you to go through the training and get up to speed as soon as possible."

"A CapCom? Great!" I thought about the many CapCom voices I'd heard during my mission, each of them an astronaut who'd flown before me. These people provided guidance, key information, and, most important, comfort. They were the friendly voices in your ear linking you with home while you floated in outer space.

My experience as CapCom lasted a grand total of twenty-four hours. The day after I met with Bob, I received another call, this time from George Abbey, the center director. George had been involved in the space program since the beginning. Originally a U.S. Air Force pilot, he had become the director of Johnson Space Center in 1996 and was already playing a critical role in keeping the space station construction on schedule. If Bob represented the corner office, George was on the top floor. Needless to say, he was one of the last people I was expecting a call from. Perhaps he wanted to talk to me about returning the items from Wales I flew on Neurolab?

George and I had always got along. He was also of Welsh descent, and he looked it—his square, imposing shoulders were built for the rugby pitch.

"Congratulations, Dafydd," George said when I got to his office. He always used the Welsh version of my name. "How are you feeling since your mission?"

"It took a few days to get my strength back, but I'm great now," I said. *George didn't ask me here just to chat about Neurolab,* I thought. *What is this really about?*

"I understand you've been assigned as a CapCom for your post-flight assignment."

"That's right. I just started yesterday."

"It's good that you're not too far into it, because now I have a special request to ask of you. Dafydd, I was wondering if you'd be willing to be the director of the Space and Life Sciences Directorate."

After a pause I said, "Thanks for considering me, George. What does it entail, and can I take on a role like that as a Canadian astronaut?"

"Don't worry," he said. "Dan Goldin has discussed this with Mac Evans and has his support."

The NASA administrator had already spoken to the president of the CSA about this? My mind was reeling. Clearly this had been in the works for a while.

George went on. "You'd be directly reporting to me and would be in charge of all the space science, life science, and space medicine programs, as well as the flight medicine clinic here at JSC. Also, we're working closely with Baylor College of Medicine to start a new life science research institute that will be called the National Space Biomedical Research Institute, so you'll be working with Dr. Bobby Alford to oversee its creation."

This was not a typical collateral duty assignment. I would have a team of some of the most talented researchers and physicians at NASA, have an opportunity to help create a new research institute, and help establish the protocols and equipment we needed to care for crews on the International Space Station. It was intimidating, but I was smart enough to know you don't say no when your boss's boss gives you an opportunity like this.

"It would be an honor," I said.

"You'll have an excellent deputy director. John Rummel will be working with you. John has extensive experience with life science and bioastronautics, and he knows the directorate well. I'll make the formal announcement, but in the meantime perhaps you could give John a call."

"I'll do that. Thanks very much." I rose and shook George's hand and left his office still not quite sure what I was taking on. His assistant, Mary, gave me a big smile as I walked past her desk and said, "I'm looking forward to working with you."

When I got back to my office, the first thing I did was pull out the NASA directory and look up who worked in the life sciences directorate. The list went on and on. I put the book down and blinked a few times to clear my head, and then I picked up the phone to tell Cathy the news.

"That's quite the promotion!" Cathy said. "Are you excited?" I could hear she was tentative but putting on a show for me. She didn't quite know what this meant, just as I hadn't. "Won't this assignment take you out of training and into management?"

"It will," I said. "But I'll still be able to fly the T-38, do space walk training, and take part in sims, even though it might not be as often as before."

I paused for a moment before continuing. "This is a huge responsibility. I'll be managing all the space and life science work at JSC, as well as the health of astronauts in space."

"You'll do fine. I'm more concerned about how you'll be able to get back to being assigned to another mission," Cathy said. "In the meantime, it sounds like this is quite an opportunity, and I'm sure it will all work out."

"It looks like I have an incredible team. Much bigger than any I've led before."

"Why do you think you and the crew did so well in space?"

I thought about it for a minute, wondering where Cathy was going with this. "We trusted each other," I said. "We knew that, no matter what, we would do our part and we could trust that others would do the same. Probably the same way you and your captain work together."

"Exactly. What was it you told me once? 'The power of the team is greater than the power of the individual.' Bring that attitude to this new job, and you'll be able to do anything."

I hadn't realized she'd been listening so carefully to things I'd said. "Thanks," I replied before bringing up my next concern. "This might mean that we'll have to be in Houston longer than we expected. Will that work?"

"My commute isn't that bad," Cathy said. My heart burst with gratitude.

"Do you think the kids will be okay with it?" I asked.

"The kids are young. This is the only home they've really known. If they finish elementary school here, we can look at heading back to Canada by the time they're ready for high school. That gives us a few years here for you to do this job and get reassigned to another flight."

After that, I drove to the Johnson Space Center to meet my new team. My office was on the eighth floor of building 1, the center's head-quarters building. As I entered the directorate office, my new executive assistant came to greet me.

"Hi, I'm Diana," she said. "If there's anything you need, don't hes-itate to ask. John Rummel asked me to let him know when you arrived. I've set up a meeting for the two of you to get together later today."

"I really appreciate it. Thanks a lot," I replied. "Perhaps we could sit down with the senior team at the same time? I've been looking for-ward to meeting them." And with that, my NASA senior leadership journey started.

I spent the morning of my first day setting up my new office. The first thing I did was put a Canadian flag in the corner. While I was now in a senior executive role at NASA, I was still a Canadian astronaut and employee of the Canadian Space Agency. It was obvious that there had been a few conversations between George Abbey; Dan Goldin, the NASA administrator; and Mac Evans, the president of the Canadian Space Agency, to make this happen, and I didn't want to disappoint anyone. In fact, for me, this opportunity reinforced the most import-ant story of the International Space Station: the power of international collaboration.

The top shelf of the bookcase beside my desk had what looked like an intercom speaker on it. "What's that for?" I asked Diana.

"It's connected to Mission Control so you can listen to air-to-ground when the shuttle's in space," she said. I was glad to know that although I wouldn't be flying on a mission anytime soon, I would never be far away from the action. Clearly the NASA safety culture was based on keeping top leaders engaged in mission operations.

The remainder of the bookshelf was bare and I wondered what to put on it. At the bottom of one box I found the model of the Avro Arrow that had traveled with me ever since Cathy and I moved to Mon-tréal. The Avro Arrow was a Canadian fighter jet that had been built in the 1950s; at the time, it was the most advanced interceptor in the world. The project was scrapped, but in many ways it was a precursor to other supersonic aircraft and, in some ways, it influenced the design of the shuttle I'd just ridden into space. Many of the Avro engineers were hired by NASA after cancellation of the Arrow project and played key engineering roles in the development of the Mercury, Gemini, and Apollo spacecraft.

Incredible to think of how far we've come, I thought.

Now I knew what to put on the bare spot of that shelf. I placed the Avro Arrow on it, then continued to rummage through other boxes, unpacking books, training manuals, and old checklists from the Neurolab mission. None of it seemed important enough for the top shelf. In a few months, though, the model of the Arrow would be joined by a photograph. This was not an everyday photograph of family or friends. This was a photograph given to me by Dave McKay, one of the scientists on the space science team. In 1996, Dave and a team from JSC were studying a meteorite from Mars known as Allan Hills 84001. They discovered evidence that suggested there were microbial fossils in the meteorite. *Ancient life on Mars,* I thought with excitement when I first read their findings. I put the photo on the shelf, right beside the Avro Arrow. *The Making Impossible Possible Shelf,* I thought. *That's what I'll call it.*

When I started my role as the life sciences director, NASA was preparing for the launch of the first elements of the space station. It was an international project that had been years in the making, so naturally there was a whirlwind of activity. Pulling it off was a challenge unlike any other, but the possibilities of the station seemed limitless.

One of the first meetings I attended in my new role was what people called a GASR: a George Abbey Saturday Review. George was the only one that could get everyone together at the same time to resolve issues, especially when the only time everyone had free was on the weekend. At 8:00 a.m., I walked into a room crowded with NASA staff, with contractors and representatives from other international agencies joining by teleconference. The entire international space community was represented in that room, and at the center of it all was George.

The first space station module, Zarya, was scheduled to launch on a Proton rocket in November, barely five months away. The Unity module, or node 1, was scheduled for delivery a month later on the space shuttle. The first crew would arrive in July 2000 after the Russian Zvezda module was added. With more than forty assembly flights required to build the space station, the schedule was aggressive, tightly integrated, and intolerant of delay. If anyone could coordinate the efforts of five international partners and keep everyone on schedule, it was George Abbey.

The issue of the day was cooling systems. In the past, there had been a coolant loop leak on the Russian *Mir* station and chemicals had leaked inside the module. The goal for the ISS was to eliminate the use of toxic materials inside the station wherever possible.

"I understand the Russians use a different coolant from us," George said to me. "Is it toxic? Do you know what is in it?"

"I've been told that it is not toxic, but I don't know yet what the coolant is exactly," I said.

"We'll have to know before we send the crew. Let me know if you have any difficulty getting the information."

There were thousands of such details that needed to be resolved before we launched each part of the ISS. It was a nonstop parade of multicultural teams across the globe working together solving problem after problem.

It was all worth it when I watched Yuri Gidzenko, Sergei Krikalev, and Bill "Shep" Shepherd lift off from Baikonur on October 31, 2000. They were the first crew to fly to the ISS, the beginning of a continuous human presence in space. My team had worked hard with Russian flight surgeons to help keep them healthy and safe in the lead-up to their mission. Flying to space myself had been a thrill, but helping enable a whole new era of space travel was exciting on an entirely different level. As *Soyuz TM-31* and its crew took off for their first flight to the ISS, it seemed that the hopes for our future in space were lifting off with them.

Will NASA ever create a model of the station that I can fit on my shelf? I wondered.

I had come to realize that the urge to explore was a fundamental part of who I was. I'd temporarily traded spaceflight for a different challenge, running a massive organization with a large budget and a team of over 1,000 people. Although I was home most nights, my schedule was actually more demanding than when I was training for Neurolab. If Cathy was flying on the weekend, I would bring Evan and Olivia with me to the astronaut gym for my workouts. While I was lifting weights, they'd be playing basketball. For us, flying in space was a family affair.

By 2001, NASA was well into space station construction, with expedition crews rotating on the ISS every few months. The length and complexity of the missions were increasing, and astronaut training had to adapt to meet it. The training for long-duration crews evolved, pulling in unconventional activities like sending crews to train with the National Outdoor Leadership School to learn about expeditionary behavior.

It was around that time that Mike Gernhardt, an astronaut, professional diver, and expert in the physiology of decompression sickness, called to set up a meeting.

Mike was incredibly creative. He was constantly thinking outside the box, so when he said he wanted to talk about an idea involving an underwater habitat, I knew I had to hear it. He and Bill Todd, a simulation supervisor whom I had met a number of times in shuttle simulation exercises, came to my office to explain their idea.

They were barely through the door when Mike launched into his pitch.

"Dave, we should be using the undersea research habitat for our training," he said.

"Sounds good. What are you suggesting?" I asked.

"The National Oceanic and Atmospheric Administration operates the world's only undersea research laboratory off the coast of Key Largo," Bill said. "It's called Aquarius. It would be an ideal environment to train astronauts for missions to the space station, and we could also use it to evaluate potential lunar missions or missions to Mars."

"How so?" I asked.

"We can weigh the divers out to be neutrally buoyant to simulate space walks around the ISS, or we can weigh them down to walk on the seabed, mimicking lunar or Martian gravity."

"It's a perfect substitute for space," Mike added, his smile broadening. "It will be a huge benefit for astronauts who haven't gone to space yet. If they can practice in a confined environment underwater for long stretches, they'll be able to adapt to living on the space station that much faster. We can also use it to test out technology and experiments that we might use on the ISS."

It wouldn't be the first time that underwater and space exploration came together. In 1965, after his Mercury spaceflight, Scott Carpenter went to work with the U.S. Navy on the Sealab missions, spending twenty-eight days living on the ocean floor off the coast of California. NASA had always done underwater training to prepare astronauts for space walks, but those had only been in a pool. Aquarius was a big step up, and it would take a lot of work and planning, but they were right: the payoff would be worth it. *Expand our thinking, and we can expand our horizons,* I thought.

"I like it," I said. "Sounds like a fantastic idea. Will NOAA let us use the habitat?"

"That shouldn't be a problem," Bill said. "They are already using it collaboratively with the navy and university researchers."

"Imagine, two major government agencies working together. Go for it and let me know what support you'll need."

A few months later, NEEMO (NASA Extreme Environment Mission Operations) was born. The name acknowledged the famous submarine captain in Jules Verne's *Twenty Thousand Leagues Under the Sea*. Mike and Bill had put their heads together and came up with a plan for a weeklong test mission underwater on Aquarius.

"Did you have any suggestions for the crew?" I asked Mike and Bill during one of the early planning sessions. "There have to be two habitat technicians, so that leaves four spots for NASA."

"Since it's a test mission," Bill said, "we were thinking the three of us, with Mike 'L.A.' as the fourth." Mike López-Alegría—or L.A., as he was called in the office—had led the ISS crew operations office and had just flown an ISS assembly mission.

I was thrilled with the idea. I'd already realized my childhood dream of becoming an astronaut, but the opportunity to live underwater and become an aquanaut, too, seemed too good to pass up. If I was going to participate, though, I had to get the all clear from George.

George listened carefully while I explained all the details and rationalized the plan. He was taking it all in, but his quiet demeanor was a bit disconcerting.

"Are there valid scientific and research objectives?" George asked when I'd finished my pitch.

It was a good question, one that Mike, Bill, and I had discussed at length. "That's what we want to find out," I said. "I think there may be a number, but we'll see."

"I suppose you'll want to be a part of this mission?" George asked.

This was the moment I'd been worrying about. I really wanted to be a part of the mission but also did not want to appear self-serving. "It looks like a reasonable training equivalent to a space mission," I said. "I think it would be good for me to be there to see firsthand whether or not we can use it for space life science experiments."

George raised an eyebrow. He could tell how excited I was. I felt myself starting to sweat. I could see my dream of underwater explorations washing away on a giant wave. "I'd like a full report after the mission," he said. "Have you spoken with Jim and Charlie?" Jim Wetherbee was the director of the Flight Crew Operations Directorate and

Charlie Precourt was the new head of the Astronaut Office, and since three astronauts would be participating, it was important to have their support.

"They like the idea of a test mission. We all want to see what we learn before committing to an ongoing program," I said.

"Okay, keep me in the loop."

I couldn't believe it. "Thanks!" I said, trying to temper my enthusiasm. "It'll be an interesting mission. Thank you, George!" I went back to my office and asked Diana to set up a follow-up meeting with Mike and Bill. There was a lot to do to get ready. *If we do this right, it could be a whole new frontier for NASA,* I thought as I contemplated the Avro Arrow on my shelf.

Unlike spaceflight, the training for NEEMO-1 took place the week before the mission. It had been a couple of years since I'd been to space, but on the morning I had to say good-bye to Evan and Olivia, it felt as though I'd only just come home.

"Are you going back to space, Daddy?" Olivia asked.

"Not this time," I said. "I'm going underwater."

"Like Ariel?" she asked. Olivia had been going through a big Disney phase the past year.

"Exactly. I'm going to live at the bottom of the ocean. But just for a little while."

Olivia shivered. "But it's cold underwater."

"Yes, it is. Why don't you give me a hug to keep me warm?"

I held both kids close, then stood to say good-bye to Cathy.

"I feel like we're getting used to this," I joked.

"We'll never get used to saying good-bye," Cathy said. "At least this time there's no rocket for me to worry about."

"And it's only two weeks," I added.

We flew down to Miami and drove a couple of hours south to Key Largo to start training. The habitat technicians didn't care how much diving experience we had: they needed to see us prove ourselves in the water. We went through the same scuba tests I'd done when I first got

Training for the NEEMO mission to Aquarius brought me back to my first experiences with SCUBA diving as a twelve-year-old. The gear had come a long way since then. *Right photo courtesy of NASA*

certified as a kid, as well as lectures on the habitat systems and experiments we'd be running. The habitat technicians took care of most of the detailed work on the station, but, as one of them half joked, "We need to make sure you don't turn a valve the wrong way and blow up the pressure system."

Throughout our training, we dove several times through the surrounding reef to familiarize ourselves with the environment. Aquarius wasn't the only man-made structure on the reef. Dotted around the seabed were a series of way stations with high-pressure fill points; we called them gazebos. From the outside they resembled upside-down barrels. When you swam into them from the bottom, you popped up into an air pocket, allowing you to talk to a fellow diver, use a radio to speak to the habitat, or refill your tanks. We learned how to navigate from the station to the way stations and out into the reef beyond, each sandbar and coral formation imprinting itself on our mental map. We followed a series of excursion lines or ropes suspended from the bottom to ensure we always knew how to get back to the habitat.

After our training was complete, we spent the weekend getting our things together and resting before heading out for the mission itself. The descent to the station was the exact opposite of my flight to space. The noise, heat, and speed of the rocket were replaced with the cool, quiet embrace of the ocean. There were no television stations filming us and we didn't have a climactic countdown—just the dive boat with a small crew waving at us as we swam beneath the surface. *What goes down eventually comes up,* I thought as I released the air from my buoyancy compensator and inhaled the first of the many breaths underwater that I would take that week.

Aquarius resembled a large RV camper underwater: it was big, long, and yellow. Each side rectangular, with windows on all sides. It stood on four legs above the seabed and the entrance was at one end. To get into it, we swam underneath the edge of the habitat, where there was a metal grate that allowed us to stand up. The pressure inside prevented the water from entering the habitat itself, so we stood on the grate, waist-deep in water, and removed our dive equipment, hanging it on hooks on the walls around us before climbing up a ladder into the wet porch, the first section of the habitat that led into the main living area.

The habitat technicians had made it clear during our training that the wet porch was to stay wet and the interior of the habitat had to stay dry. We ditched the last of our wet gear outside and had a quick rinse off—"Navy showers only," the technicians had warned us, meaning two minutes or less—then headed into the habitat's living quarters.

We toweled dry and passed around eardrops—the 100 percent humidity in the lab meant that each of us had a huge risk of getting an ear infection if we weren't proactive—as we looked over our new home. An entire wall of the main room was covered with valves and communication equipment, and opposite it was the galley, with a kitchen sink, fridge, and microwave. The kitchen table looked like something you'd find in a trailer, and above it was a huge window that often attracted crowds of curious fish looking in at each meal. At the far end was a door that led into the bunks, three of them stacked on either side of the room, with a viewing port in the wall at the end.

"I'll take a low bunk," Mike said.

"Me, too," Bill said.

At least the view will be better from the top bunk, I thought.

The plan was for us to spend the week conducting experiments both inside and outside the habitat, following a mission timeline identical to a spaceflight. It surprised me how quickly I fell back into my spaceflight mode.

"Is anyone else already tired of the space food?" I asked the first morning at breakfast.

"I'm happy to switch to whatever Otter and Ryan are eating," Mike said, referring to the two habitat technicians who were enjoying fresh food from the local supermarket that had been sent down to the habitat.

"We have interesting neighbors," I said, looking out the viewing port as a reef shark swam past. Later that evening, as I lay in my bunk, I reflected on the differences between living in space and living underwater. At night, the external habitat lights cast a bluish glow into the surrounding water. The viewing port was surrounded by reef fish of every color, and every now and then a barracuda would swim past. Whether in space or under the sea, the majestic beauty of our planet was something I came to cherish more with each mission.

The next day we were planning a dive along one of the excursion lines. Getting lost would be catastrophic, so we followed the ropes with the same rigor we would use with our tethers in a space walk. While we were documenting parts of the reef where the coral had died, Dr. Steve Miller and Dr. Joe MacInnis swam over to say hello. Steve was the Aquarius scientific director, and Joe was Canada's most famous diving physician, whose exploits had captured my imagination as a child. Somehow it seemed fitting that the first time I met Joe would be on a reef sixty feet beneath the ocean's surface.

We quickly settled into a rhythm and daily routine. We dove at least twice a day, so our wetsuits were never dry. After the first day, it seemed like a new member had joined our crew. I swam up into the wet porch after one of our dives, and a few feet in front of me I saw a large barracuda swimming close by.

I tried to shoo the fish back into the open water, but it just swam out of reach. It seemed content to simply hang out in the wet porch.

"What are we going to do about that barracuda?" I asked the others when we were back inside the habitat.

"Just leave him," Mike said. "He'll probably swim away on his own.

But he didn't. The fish was still there when we left for our next dive, and again when we got back. He was totally benign. Before long, we started calling him Bob—Big Old Barracuda—and we'd simply brush him out of the way when we wanted to get into the water.

Our night dives were my favorite part. The reef that was our temporary home looked entirely different in the dark. Before leaving the habitat, we would double-check all of our equipment: flashlights, strobe lights, and tether reels. Each buddy pair attached a different-colored fluorescent stick to the top of their tanks so that it was easy to identify each other. Bill and I had red, and the Mike's had green. The four of us swam out along the southeast excursion line into the bluish-black mist beyond the habitat's lights. When we were eighty feet deep, we attached our tethers to the line and swam down into a sandy patch on the bottom of the ocean. We all turned our flashlights off and lay there, looking into the blackness. The biophosphorescent plankton surrounded us like millions of fireflies on a summer's evening, while the moon cast a shimmering light through the water. I felt as if I were completely alone in the universe, suspended in a world of my own. After several minutes we realized it was time to swim back to the habitat. The lights of Aquarius glowed in the distance, a light blue halo surrounding our home in the ocean.

Of course, despite our best efforts, sometimes unexpected things happened during a mission. When we got back to the habitat, we discovered that the video camera seemed to have water in the housing. Inside the camera was soaking wet. Instead of just scrapping it, we decided to try to rescue it. We grabbed a hairdryer to dry it. The only problem was that we forgot to look at the intake on the hairdryer before we started it. There was a mixture of hair and dust in it, and we were using it longer than we normally did when we dried our ears. We didn't anticipate it overheating, but the next thing we knew, there was smoke billowing out of the dryer. We unplugged it immediately, but it was too late: it had triggered the smoke alarm.

The sensors were designed to be incredibly responsive to any bit of smoke. The ironic part of living underwater was that fire was one of our greatest fears. The lab's safety regulations indicated that if a fire wasn't immediately contained, we would have to evacuate by swimming to the gazebo beside the habitat, where we'd call and wait for a dive boat. We'd then have to swim to the surface, knowingly giving ourselves the bends; then we'd be brought back to shore and placed in a hyperbaric chamber. Needless to say, none of us wanted to do that.

The six of us raced to put on our breathing systems and followed the emergency procedure checklist. Thankfully, there were no flames and the puff of smoke was short-lasting so we wouldn't have to leave. Our lead hab-tech, Otter, was speaking with the topside team on the radio, discussing what had happened.

Even though there had been no flames, the event was recorded in the log as "A brief pyrolytic event involving a hairdryer. No damage to the station and no one is hurt."

A pause and the topside team called back asking: "How's your hair?" We later found out that the topside team had planned a simulated power failure for us the next morning, but they canceled it after we created our own emergency.

My final night in the station, I lay in my bunk, listening to the many noises of the habitat while looking out the viewing port at the fish once more. I thought back to what I'd told Olivia before I left: "I'm going to live at the bottom of the ocean." I said it again to myself, wondering if stating the obvious could make it less remarkable; it couldn't. I thought back to the first conversation Mike, Bill, and I had about the mission; it had seemed like a pipe dream. I imagined other undersea explorers who might follow in the footsteps of Aquarius aquanauts and the things they might accomplish and create that we could barely imagine.

Then an image came into my mind: that photo of my dad after he had climbed to the peak of a mountain as a young man, resting and scanning the horizon for the next summit. I was not on a mountaintop, but as I fell asleep, one thought echoed in my mind: *Dad, I know exactly how you felt.*

12

The Gift of Life

When I resurfaced for the first time from our NEEMO mission, I bobbed in the water, looked up at the sky, and thought, *I need to go back to space.* After all of the post-mission debriefs were complete, I turned my attention to getting reassigned to another flight. I had high hopes for another mission as an astronaut.

It's easy to be positive when things are going well. When you finish a day of training, having flown a NASA T-38 through crystal clear skies, or when you lie down in your bunk in the space shuttle and look out at the earth passing beneath you, it's easy to think that the good times will go on uninterrupted. But life doesn't always give us an easy path. It's when we hit a wall or face an unforeseen challenge that our determination is tested. Setbacks may slow us down, but they don't have to stop us.

In late 2002, I gave up my role as director of space and life science to be assigned to a mission. I was joining the crew of STS-118, and we were scheduled to fly to the International Space Station the next winter. At least, that was the plan. We had several months of training ahead of us. I had kept up my training in the simulators and classrooms when I was the director of life sciences, but I still had a lot to catch up on. For one thing, this would be my first trip to the space station, so I needed to learn new systems. I was also scheduled to perform a number of space walks during this next mission. I'd finally be able to hone the skills I'd learned and practiced for years! I was prepared to spend most of 2003 in one form of training or another and a lot of it would be at NASA's underwater training facility, the Neutral Buoyancy Laboratory. In the meantime, there were other missions that were scheduled to fly, the first of which was STS-107.

After a successful launch and mission, on February 1, 2003, the space shuttle *Columbia* was to return from its fifteen-day mission. I was at home watching the reentry on NASA TV with Cathy, the kids, and some friends who were visiting from Toronto. At 9:00 a.m., mission control lost communication with the orbiter as it was passing over northern Texas. It was immediately obvious something was wrong. Images began to appear of the vehicle breaking apart in the upper atmosphere and my cell phone rang. It was Rich Williams, the chief medical officer of NASA, calling from Washington.

"Are you watching the reentry?" Rich asked.

"Yes," I said. "It looks like we've lost *Columbia*. I'm on my way to JSC and I'll call you from there."

"Okay," Rich said. "We'll talk soon."

As I drove to the center, my thoughts were occupied with the magnitude of the tragedy. Rick Husband and the rest of the *Columbia* crew—Willie McCool, Mike Anderson, Kalpana Chawla, Dave Brown, Laurel Blair Salton Clark, Ilan Ramon—were our friends and colleagues. Rick, Mike, and Kalpana had been my classmates. We'd spent hundreds of hours together in simulations, seminars, and training sessions. I'd been looking forward to sitting down with them over a cold beer and hearing stories of their mission. Now neither their families nor any of us would ever see them again.

I felt every bit of warmth drain from me. They were only a few minutes away from landing safely—a few minutes from reuniting with their families.

I went straight to the eighth floor of building 1, my old office, to see if there was anything I could do to be of assistance. Jeffrey R. Davis, my successor, was already there with the life sciences team reviewing what had been done so far and what would need to be done over the ensuing days.

"Anything I can do to help?" I asked Jeff.

"No, thanks. We're just going through the protocol."

"I'll head over to the astronaut office and give you a call later," I said.

Within a couple of hours I was in northeastern Texas. The space shuttle fleet had been immediately grounded indefinitely until NASA could figure out what had happened and correct the problem. The recovery of the shuttle wreckage was vital to that analysis, and the efforts of state and federal agencies were coordinated with NASA personnel in the field. The debris was spread across much of northeastern Texas, and it was critical to secure all of it as quickly as possible. Jim Wetherbee, the former director of the Flight Crew Operations Directorate, George "Zambo" Zamka, and Barry "Butch" Wilmore drove with me to Lufkin, Texas, to help coordinate the recovery efforts.

Jim, Zambo, and Butch went to the command center to start working with FEMA and local authorities. I went to work with the FBI to help coordinate crew recovery. In mid-fall 2002, I had asked Phil Stepaniak, one of the NASA flight surgeons, to update the plan we would use for crew recovery if we lost a space shuttle. Little did I know that within six months we'd be using it. After explaining who I was and why I was there to the two FBI evidence response team members, we quickly got down to work implementing the plan. Using local facilities, everything fell into place, and by the time we were finished, it was one in the morning. I didn't have a motel room or other place to stay, so I slept on the floor of the office that became my home for the next three days. *I can't leave them alone,* I thought. Somehow it seemed appropriate that I be there with my fallen colleagues, a fellow astronaut who understood their commitment and what it had cost them.

The next day I went over to the command center for the briefing on the daily search plan. In the lobby, there was an elderly couple who had driven from out of state to see if volunteers were needed.

"If you go over to that desk on the far side of the lobby," I said to them, "they'll see if there is something you can help with." Later that day I went back to the command center for a quick check-in and saw the couple, each of them wearing name tags and safety vests. They were sweeping the lobby. Their compassion and selflessness touched my heart.

While the tragic loss of our friends hung over us every minute, at the same time something incredible was happening. The response was America at its finest. Volunteers from the U.S. Forestry Service arrived from all over the United States to help search the dense woods of northeastern Texas. Literally every branch of the government was represented: FEMA, the FBI, the EPA, Texas State Troopers, the Texas National Guard, and more than sixty other agencies—while volunteers and private groups provided personnel, supplies, and equipment.

We clearly understood the magnitude of what lay ahead, and we also recognized that we still had astronauts—Ken "Sox" Bowersox, Don Pettit, and Nikolai Budarin—on the space station who needed our support. Despite the loss, everyone at NASA picked themselves up and made sure the day-to-day station operations continued flawlessly. It was a truly inspiring "badgeless" effort where everyone worked together. Months later, when the recovery was finished, it was determined that searchers combed the equivalent of a forty-foot-wide swath to the moon and back.

After three days in the field, I returned to Johnson Space Center for a mandatory rest period. With no distractions to keep me busy, the stark reality of losing seven friends hit me hard. My first day back, I passed a crowd of people laying wreaths in a makeshift memorial along the sign outside the center's main entrance. I felt a lump in my throat that I had to swallow down. I attended the funeral ceremonies of my friends and the ceremony at JSC and listened to the words of President Bush: "This cause of exploration and discovery is not an option we choose. It is a desire written in the human heart . . . We find the best among us, send them forth into unmapped darkness, and pray they will return. They go in peace for all mankind, and all mankind is in their debt." There is no question that the crew of STS-107 represented the best among us. It was hard to let them go, but in my heart I knew they would want us to continue to explore, to go farther, stay longer, and leave human footsteps on another planet.

A few days later, on my way back to the *Columbia* wreckage site again, I thought about a patient I'd treated years before in the emergency ward. He was a pilot, and when I heard his helicopter had plummeted from the sky, I expected the worst. Instead, I was greeted by a fully conscious patient with only a few scratches and a twisted ankle. I saw photos of the helicopter later, and it was completely wrecked. *How did he walk away from that?* I thought.

I wondered why that helicopter pilot had been spared but my friends hadn't. It struck me that risk is everywhere. There are risks to everything in life. I had jumped into the car that morning without a second thought, but the truth is that an accident can happen on a highway as easily as it can to a helicopter pilot or a space shuttle crew. The loss of my friends on *Columbia* was a sobering reminder that every moment mattered, and that I could never become complacent about the gift of life.

When word finally came down that our mission had been rescheduled, I experienced a mix of emotions. I was excited that, after implementing the recommendations of the *Columbia* Accident Investigation

Board, we'd be returning to flight, but the loss of *Columbia* led to a lot of reflection. I did what I always do in such situations: I turned to Cathy.

"We won't launch for another three or four years," I said after we'd put the kids to sleep. "They'll have lots of time to make improvements and implement the board's recommendations. I'd like to go fly again."

Cathy gave a small smile. "We've always trusted each other to make the right decisions," she replied. "You know that every time I step into the cockpit, there's no place I'd rather be, and you trust that I'll do everything I can to come back safely."

"And you know I do the same."

"Of course. I would never make this decision for you. The decision is yours, and no matter what you do, we'll figure it out together as a family."

I talked with others on the crew, and we were all in similar states of mourning and contemplation. We'd been delivered a stark reminder of how short life could be, but we also knew we were part of something bigger. We had good reason to be afraid and ask ourselves, *Do we go back and do this again?* But to be courageous is to accept the fact that you're afraid and still do what it is you fear doing. Time was helping to heal our wounds, and ultimately we all agreed we would serve on the mission together. We believed that the friends we lost on STS-107, the astronauts of *Challenger*, and the *Apollo 1* astronauts who perished in a capsule fire during a launch rehearsal would have wanted us to continue—to continue their legacy and live as they had lived, pushing the limits of human space exploration. It would dishonor their memory to stop flying.

In May 2004, I went in for my annual medical checkup to maintain my flight status as an astronaut and pilot. We were constantly going in for medicals throughout our training, so I was now more comfortable entering the doctor's office as a patient rather than a physician.

"Dave, your fiftieth birthday is coming up," Joe Schmid, one of the flight surgeons, said. "Do you have any special plans for your birthday?"

"Cathy and I are going to the Simon and Garfunkel concert," I said. Diana, my former assistant, had given me two tickets as a birthday present.

"That'll be fun."

The medical was uneventful. There was the standard blood work and a few other tests, but I looked to be in good shape and was still getting to the gym at least five times a week as part of my space walk training.

We reviewed the test results a couple of days later. The moment Joe walked into the room, I knew something wasn't right. He caught me watching him.

"I know I can't hide anything from you," Joe said. "I'll get right to the point. The test results showed that your PSA levels are a little high."

PSAs are antigens that occur naturally in the body. A higher count can be a sign of prostate cancer, but there are other things that can cause an elevated PSA. The doctor in me wanted to remain rational and not jump to conclusions. But the patient side of me needed reassurance.

"What do you think we should do?" I asked.

Joe gave the standard answer, exactly the one I would have given if our roles had been reversed. "Let's repeat the test and see if it's still elevated. It might just be a false positive."

The technician came in and drew the blood specimen that would ultimately change my future. I tried to ignore the dark cloud hanging over that momentous birthday.

At the concert that evening, Simon and Garfunkel sounded just like they had when I first heard them years earlier. As Cathy and I listened to them play "America," I remembered the first time I played the song for her on the guitar. Would my whole life soon change? What would the future bring?

"I know you're worried," Cathy said, giving my hand a squeeze. "We can't control what might happen. It's a beautiful concert, so let's enjoy this moment."

I smiled and squeezed back, then returned my attention to the music and lost myself in the songs of my youth. Later that night, I went in to see Olivia and Evan sound asleep in their beds and gave them each a little hug.

Over the next few weeks I carried on with training as normal—with intermittent visits to the flight medicine clinic between. I went from a training simulation to having a biopsy done, from space walk practice to the clinic for updates. The worry hung over me the entire time. The uncertainty was the hardest part. Finally, Joe had enough information to make a definitive diagnosis.

I got the call early one morning, "I'm sorry, Dave, but the news isn't good," he said. "You have prostate cancer."

Nobody wants to be a member of the cancer club. But for those of us who do join it, I suspect we all have the exact same first thought: *I'm going to die.* When I heard those words "You have prostate cancer," I wasn't a doctor or an astronaut anymore. I was just a scared human being who felt like he'd been handed a death sentence.

Cathy had heard the news, as I had held the phone away from my ear. She reached out to hold my hand and gave it a squeeze. "You'll get through this; *we'll* get through this."

Everything was put on hold. We were still several years out from our flight for STS-118, but I was scheduled to be the commander of the next NEEMO mission to Aquarius in just a couple of months. I knew that a medical review board would wait until after surgery to see if I was fit for spaceflight, let alone lead an underwater mission. So I tried to keep my goals simple: to get through surgery and hopefully remove all of the tumor, recover as quickly as possible, and get back to flight status.

I went into action, researching prostate cancer and talking with experts. I tried to learn every last detail that I could about the disease and the possible treatments. As long as I approached my cancer as a doctor, I felt I could control it.

It was harder for Cathy. "It's like watching you fly to space again,"

When I was diagnosed with prostate cancer, my first thoughts were of moments like this with Evan and Olivia, and how I would do anything to be with them.

she said. "But take everything you experience, multiply it by ten, and that's what it's like to watch from the outside."

"I never thought about it that way," I admitted.

"Has NASA found you a surgeon yet?"

"They have. His name is Dr. Peter Scardino," I said. "He's one of the best. The only catch is that he works at Memorial Sloan Kettering in New York City."

"New York? That might be a bit far to bring the kids."

"I was thinking about that," I said. "You could leave the kids with Maria and come up for the surgery, then head back right after, if you like. I want nothing more than to be with you and the kids, but I don't want them to have to see me in recovery, and it's not fair to you to travel alone for so long with them. I'll have the surgery, recover for a few days, and then we can all be home together."

"Are you sure? I don't love the idea of you being in the hospital and recovering alone."

"Just think of it like a mission," I said. "I'll be back before you know it."

Cathy agreed, and we decided she would fly up with me. My surgery was scheduled for August 2004. When I was admitted to the hospital, the nurse led me to a small room and handed me a little blue gown.

"Go in and put this on," she said. "Just so you know, it opens up at the back." Yes, I knew that, but regardless, it was odd to have the roles reversed. I folded my clothes neatly and left them on a chair, then pulled on the gown. I sat down on the stretcher and rubbed my arms to warm myself up. The nurse reentered a few minutes later and paused when she saw me sitting on the stretcher.

"Please lie down," she said. "The handrails must be up at all times." I slowly lay back, realizing that, somewhere between sitting up and lying down, I had gone from being a physician-astronaut to becoming a patient. Recently, in health care, there has been a lot of discussion about finding a different word to use instead of "patient." Some argue patients should be called "clients." Others prefer "people" or "person." But I still prefer "patient." To me, being a patient means I'm not at my best, that there is a reason why I need care, compassion, respect, and dignity. The moment I lay down on that stretcher, I became vulnerable. I began to see health care from a totally different perspective.

Cathy and Jean-Marc Comtois, my Canadian flight surgeon, were there with me as I got settled waiting for the operation. We said goodbye—a hug for Cathy and a handshake for Jean-Marc. As I was wheeled down the hallway, I tried to focus on the chatter of the nurses and doctors around me, but questions kept creeping into my head. Would I be cured? Would I have prostate cancer forever? What if I needed radiation? What if I wasn't there for Evan and Olivia?

Later that day, when I woke up after surgery, everything hurt. *So this is what it's like to be on the receiving end of the knife,* I thought blearily. I had a long, vertical incision in the lower part of my abdomen, and there were IVs, drains, and catheters going into and coming out of my body. I looked past the equipment to see Cathy, Jean-Marc, and my best friend, Bill Thomas, and his wife, Ursula, sitting beside me in the recovery room.

"The surgery went well," Dr. Scardino said. "I'm glad you chose an open radical procedure. After I removed the prostate, the biopsies of the lymph nodes were negative, but I found a couple of areas where the tumor had spread. I was able to do a wide excision. I think I got it all."

"Thanks," I said. What does one say to a doctor who has given you back the gift of life? Now I understood how the girl with asthma, whose life I had saved in a driveway, had felt. "I really appreciate everything you've done for me." As I had done in the past, Dr. Scardino down-played what he had done, saying, "I'm glad it worked out."

As a physician I knew what I had to do. A spirometer for breathing exercises sat on the table by the head of my bed. Taking a deep breath precipitated a wave of pain in my lower abdomen, but I did the best I could on each exercise, realizing that my recovery was up to me.

I had to get up each day for some exercise. The first time I tried to stand, I barely made it off the bed. It took me a while to roll on my side, then try and swing my legs over the bed. That was when it hurt the most, twisted to the side. I pushed myself up to a sitting position and slowly stood up. Despite running roughly thirty miles every week, my legs felt weak. I sat back down with a long sigh.

"You need to get out of bed," the nurse said as she came in to check on me.

"I know, but my legs feel weak and it hurts," I said.

She gave me an unimpressed look, the same one that I might have given Olivia if she had said "I'm tired" after two minutes in the grocery store. It was a look that said, *Suck it up.*

When the going gets tough, the tough get going, I thought. I tried again to pull myself up to stand. With each attempt, I improved. The pain was there, and it was intense, but I was upright—standing on my own two feet. I took a step, then another. I rested, tried again later. Eventually, I made it a little farther into the ward. I was only fifty years old, but I was hobbling around like I was ninety, clinging to the IV pole that held my catheter bag. The nurses would smile and greet me every time I passed their desk, and the cleaner for our floor became my unofficial coach.

"Dave, you're looking pretty good today!" he said a few days after my surgery. "Walking a little faster, I see. Keep it up!"

I flashed him a thumbs-up as I continued my laps.

The five-day admission went by quickly, and I was finally ready to be discharged. On my last day in the hospital, Dr. Scardino entered with one of the nurses.

"Dave, everything looks good," he said cheerily. "Nothing changed in the formal pathology report, so it looks like the surgery was a success. The Foley bladder catheter will stay in for two weeks. We just need to take your drains out and you'll be on your way home."

"No problem," I said, nervously watching him as he pulled on gloves and cut the sutures holding the drains in place. "I know the drill."

"Great. You might feel a little tugging inside when I pull the drain out."

I appreciated the attempt to calm me down, but it did nothing to ease the feeling of the long drain inside my abdomen being pulled out. Some adhesions had already started to form on the drains and it felt like my insides were coming with them as he pulled. It wasn't particularly painful but I was happy when it was over.

When the drains were finally out, one of the nurses remained to help me clean up and get dressed to leave.

"So you're a doctor, right?" she asked as she changed my bandages.

"Yes, I am," I said.

"Have you learned anything since you've been here?"

"Absolutely! I finally understand what it's like to be a patient."

She smiled knowingly. "You'll remember that when you're back at work, won't you?"

"I will, I promise."

I spent the next night in a hotel before heading back home to Houston. I couldn't wait to return to Cathy and the kids. I wanted nothing more than to be home with them.

We had told Evan and Olivia that I was having surgery, but not what it was for. When Evan and Olivia first saw me, they looked concerned at how slowly I was walking and the fact that I had a tube draining my bladder hooked up to a bag on my leg. Still, it was great to be back home.

"They've really missed you," Cathy said as they tried to climb on top of me and give me a careful hug.

Two weeks later I went to the Flight Medicine Clinic and Jeff Jones, another one of the flight surgeons and a urologist, checked that everything was healing well. After Jeff removed my catheter, I went to see Corey Twine, my strength and conditioning coach, to start the long road of getting back into shape. I still hoped to get back my flight certification and possibly even continue in my role as commander of NEEMO-7.

Corey looked at me and said, "We'll start slowly and work up from there. It will take time, but if you do everything I ask you to, you'll soon be back to where you were before surgery." With that he handed me a five-pound dumbbell.

"Really?" I said, looking at him with surprise.

"Yes, really. It takes time," he responded.

Corey was right. Within four weeks, with his supervision, I was back to my regular level of fitness and ready for the medical board to decide if I could participate in NEEMO-7. Postoperative certification for a saturation diving mission was a little unusual for the NASA flight surgeons. They were used to dealing with medical certification for spaceflight, but saturation diving missions were not within their typical purview. So, with Jean-Marc's approval, NASA decided to enlist the expertise of some U.S. Navy physicians who were experts in saturation diving. I would participate in the initial discussion with the board and then I was to be excused for the board decision.

The concern expressed by the diving experts was that the scar tissue where my prostate had been would put me at risk of decompression sickness. If that were to occur at the end of the NEEMO mission, it could potentially cause incontinence or impotence, neither of which were outcomes I wanted.

Ultimately, I made the decision myself. After discussing the risks with the navy experts, I decided not to do NEEMO-7. It would be better to take more time to heal. *Better to be safe than sorry,* I thought, and so the meeting finished early following my decision. Don't they say everyone loves a meeting that finishes early? It was a tough decision, but in my heart I knew it was the right one. There would be other opportunities: two years later, I would have the chance to serve as the commander of an eighteen-day NEEMO mission. It was worth the wait.

Not long after I excused myself from NEEMO-7, the CSA and NASA convened a board to review my medical fitness for spaceflight. If they gave me the green light, I would be able to step back into my role on the mission and begin training. But if they found that something didn't look right, it would be a different story.

I spoke with Joe Schmid before the review board meeting. "If possible, I'd like to get medically certified for a long-duration mission as well as shuttle flights," I said. I didn't know if I would fly a long-duration mission. If I did, then great! But if I didn't, I wanted the board to be ready for similar decisions for long-duration crew members. If this had happened to me, chances were it would happen to others.

"Great news: you're cleared for flight on 118 and for a long-duration mission in the future," Joe said over the phone the next day.

"Fantastic!" I said. "Thanks for all your help with everything." I picked up the phone to call Cathy.

"They've cleared me for flight," I said excitedly.

"That's great news," Cathy said.

"As long as the cancer stays in remission, I'll be able to continue with the STS-118 mission."

"Sounds like something worth celebrating. That's quite the belated fiftieth-birthday present."

Cathy was right. That's exactly what I'd been given: a gift. I had a second shot at life. I recognized how fortunate I was to have that, which made me wonder, *I've made it through cancer. Do I want to throw my life on the line again by flying in space?* I knew the answer right away: Yes. There was still so much that I could learn, see, and contribute. I had always tried to live my life to the fullest. I owed it to myself and to my family to take advantage of the opportunity I'd been given and turn it into something special.

After two medical reviews, it was time to tell the NEEMO-7 crew that Bob Thirsk would be stepping in as their commander. I gathered the crew to break the news to them.

"I'm afraid I have bad news," I said quietly. "The NEEMO mission will go ahead, but I won't be on it. I had to have major surgery, and I haven't been medically cleared for the mission."

I saw the shock register across their faces. I waited for the words of comfort and consolation that typically accompanied this sort of news.

"You could have told us earlier," one of the crew said.

"I'm sorry," I said. "I was really hoping to get back into shape and get medically certified for the mission, but it is better for my health and the mission if you go ahead without me."

It wasn't the response I was expecting, although, to be fair, it was pretty big news for the crew just a few weeks before the mission. Thankfully, Bob stepped in flawlessly and he and the rest of the team did an outstanding job on the mission.

I'd had a similar conversation with Scott Kelly before I went for surgery. Scott was my mission commander for STS-118, and I respected his advice as a leader and friend. Scott had considered the information and then responded thoughtfully, "There's enough time for you to have surgery and recover before our mission. If you don't have any complications after the surgery, I would think they'll approve you for the flight. What to you think? You're the doctor."

"You're right," I said. "A lot depends on how the surgery and my recovery goes."

"You'll be fine," he said. "You're tough. You'll make it through."

The more I reflected on what Scott said, the more his positive attitude rubbed off on me. I didn't want the cancer to define my life or my days. I had a family to live for and a dream to chase. Nothing had stopped me yet, so I wasn't about to let the diagnosis destroy everything I'd worked so hard to build.

I had to be realistic, though. The twin parts of my mind—the doctor and the astronaut—were inseparable. I saw flying in space as a privilege. If I had a medical condition that might affect the mission's success or add an unknown risk to the crew, I wasn't going to bias or pressure anyone to clear me to fly.

"I don't want to jeopardize the mission," I said to Scott. "I want to fly with all of you, of course, but I don't want to put anyone at risk."

"Take your time," Scott said. "First things first: Make sure you're healthy."

I appreciated Scott's candor; as a leader he was one of the most objective people I had ever worked with. He approached every challenge the same way: Evaluate the situation and find a workable solution.

I'd had my fair share of problems, evaluated them, and found a way to work through them. Now it was finally time to head back to the stars.

13

What a Wonderful World

Every spaceflight can be broken up into a series of moments, most of them indelibly imprinted in your memory. Liftoff. Becoming weightless as you leave Earth's atmosphere. A meal shared with crewmates hundreds of kilometers above the earth's surface. I see life the same way. Our days are filled with moments, some of them life changing, some of them quieter. But whether we're in a space shuttle or in an operating room or at home with loved ones, every moment is precious. When you realize that your life is a finite series of moments, the importance of living in the present becomes a matter of choice. It is easy to be complacent about how we use our time, but every minute is paramount. If you commit yourself fully to bringing your best to every event, every encounter, every experience, there are no limits to your life. If you're courageous enough to have tough conversations and take on life's challenges, you can grow as an individual. None of us knows what life will bring, but we can decide how to live the moments we have.

Nine years after I'd first flown in space, I was finally about to live my dream again. It was August 2007, and as I packed during one of my final nights at home, Cathy and I marveled at how much had changed since the last time we'd done this dance.

"Olivia had just been born last time you flew," Cathy said.

"Evan was barely old enough to understand where I'd gone," I said. "You were a first officer then; now you're a captain."

"You were cancer-free then; now you're a cancer survivor."

"And I still am."

"Do you feel differently about this mission?"

I paused. The same mix of excitement and apprehension simmered inside me, but I felt more clear-eyed the second time around. "I know what to expect," I said. "Or at least I think I do."

"How do you feel about the space walks? Are you ready?"

I had been wondering the same thing. Space walks are one of the most difficult and dangerous tasks for astronauts. "I think so. We've trained so much for it. As a team, we've worked out every detail, and we did well in the final evaluation simulation."

"Train like you fly and fly like you train," Cathy said.

Having the right mind-set helped to prepare me for the idea of spacewalking, but the hundreds of hours of training were also important. I had spent months preparing specifically for our four planned space walks with three of my crewmates: Rick Mastracchio and Tracy Caldwell, who would be flying on STS-118 with me, and Clay Anderson, who'd be flying to the ISS a few months before us and remaining there after we left.

Rick and Clay were quite a bit younger than I was, and I was determined to prove that I was fit enough and had the skills to do the job. *Time to chase perfection,* I thought to myself each time a new task was added to one of the space walks. No one wants to make a mistake in space, especially spacewalking. It is hard to have a flawless training run in the pool, so every training session was an opportunity to learn and get ready for our final performance in space. It was mentally and physically demanding. More than once, Rick, Clay, and I would climb out of suits after hours in the pool and we'd count our bruises.

"I've got at least three on each shoulder," I announced after one training run.

"I've got about the same. You're holding up pretty well for an old guy," Clay teased.

The final training test for Rick, Tracy, and me was overseen by our instructors and an instructor astronaut who had done a number of space walks. We were given one of the space walks we would ultimately do in space to complete in the pool. If, after we'd finished, the instructors and the instructor astronaut felt that they wouldn't be comfortable going out the hatch with us, or that we wouldn't complete the space walk objectives, there would be a problem.

"This is it: Let's do everything the way we've trained it," I said as we got into our suits.

"Agreed. We know what we're doing," Rick said.

"I just don't want to screw anything up."

"You won't. We'll listen to each other and to Tracy and focus on working together, just like always. We do that, and everything will be fine."

Rick was right. We did just that, and the test went off without a problem. Each of the evaluators gave us the green light, and with that, we cleared the final hurdle. By the time our launch was upon us, I felt as ready as I would ever be. I knew the risks, and I knew that I could trust Rick, Clay, and the rest of the crew with my life. If anything came up, we would handle it.

I have a picture of Cathy hugging Evan and Olivia, watching us lift off for our mission. Evan was a teenager, and Olivia was nine going on ten, so both of them were starting to understand the real risks of spaceflight. They, along with the other spouses, family members, and support astronauts, were all on the roof of the launch control center so everyone would be together in the event of an emergency. My mother, along with our extended family and friends, watched the launch from the VIP viewing area.

Cathy told me later that when she and the kids were watching the launch, Olivia said, "It'll be all right, Mom." A few years later, when Olivia was a teenager, I was giving a presentation and I asked Olivia to comment on what it's like watching your dad lift off into space, not knowing if he is going to come back or not. Cathy and I had tried to protect the kids from worries or fears, but hearing Olivia so maturely and calmly explain how she had dealt with those emotions and knowing how strong we were as a family gave me such pride then and still does to this day.

As Cathy and the kids huddled together on the rooftop, I was riding the 7.5 million pounds of combined thrust from the solid rocket boosters and the three shuttle main engines as we began our two-day journey to rendezvous and dock with the International Space Station. I knew we had fully left Earth's atmosphere when I saw the checklist in front of me begin to rise into the air. Although it was exhilarating, I breathed a sigh of relief. *I don't think I'll ever get used to that ride,* I thought.

I unbuckled myself from my seat and carefully pushed myself out of it. My body seemed to intuitively remember the last trip, because it felt as though I had been in space the month before. Using only my fingertips, I floated out of my seat on the mid-deck to start reconfiguring the shuttle. This time I was in charge of the post-insertion timeline and I didn't want to let Scott or the crew down.

Docking a spacecraft to the space station when both are traveling twenty-five times the speed of sound requires teamwork, precision, and focus. I used a handheld radar device—similar to the ones used by traffic police—to get data on the distance and closing velocity with the space station, then Barbara Morgan and I activated the docking mechanism that would secure the shuttle to the station. There were high fives around the flight deck when the latches were locked and we got the notification that we had docked successfully. Our pilot, Charlie

The International Space Station was an incredible achievement and a testament to what's possible when countries and people work together for the greater good. *Photo courtesy of NASA*

"Scorch" Hobaugh, and I went into the shuttle airlock and waited by the hatch, getting ready for the go-ahead from Mission Control for us to enter our home for the next two weeks.

It used to be said that a shuttle mission is like a sprint, and a space station mission is more like a marathon. Now, most long-duration astronauts say that station missions are more like a six-month sprint. There's still lots happening every day, and while you may have a bit more breathing room to enjoy the moments in between the work, you still feel like you're always on, twenty-four hours a day, every day of the mission.

The first night on the ISS, as I settled into my bed, I pulled out a couple of personal items that I'd packed carefully in my bag. The first was Cathy's captain's wings, which she'd earned the year before. I had flown her first set of Air Canada wings in space on board STS-90, and I wanted to bring her captain's wings with me to space as well.

The second item was a CD. I pulled on my headphones and the sounds of Louis Armstrong's "What a Wonderful World" swirled around me. It was Olivia playing it on the piano. I'd recorded the piece before I left, and I drifted off to sleep that night to the sounds of my daughter's music.

The next day was spent running experiments and getting the equipment in place for our upcoming space walk. It is hard to describe the emotions you feel before your first space walk. It's one thing to be inside a spacecraft looking out the window at the earth, but it's something else entirely when you put on a space suit and step "outside." Rick and I went to bed early the night before, hoping to get a good sleep. We slept in the space station Quest airlock with the hatch closed and the pressure lowered from the normal station operating pressure to help remove nitrogen from our bodies. Medically, space walkers have the same risk of developing decompression sickness that scuba divers do as we go from the higher pressure of the space station to the much lower pressure in our space suits. If we were to immediately go from the station pressure to the suit pressure, the nitrogen in our bodies would create bubbles of gas in our tissues similar to the ones that form in a soft drink when the cap is removed, causing the condition known as the bends. We didn't want that to happen, so we were careful to follow the protocol closely.

Despite our best intentions to get to sleep on time, Rick and I were awakened in the middle of the night by the harsh sound of the space station alarm.

"What do you think?" I asked. We were isolated in the airlock with the hatch closed. Opening the hatch would break the pre-breathe protocol and impact the start of our space walk.

"Probably a false alarm," Rick said, sounding frustrated with the interruption.

Seconds later, Mission Control confirmed Rick's suspicions. We both closed our eyes and tried the best we could to get back to sleep quickly. I found it difficult: I couldn't stop thinking about everything we had to do and the fact that now we'd be tired for our first space walk. Fortunately, I had practiced for something like this in my training by doing a couple of training runs in the pool with only three hours sleep the night before to see if fatigue would affect my performance. It took more focus, but I knew I could do it. As I mentally rehearsed the many tasks that Rick and I would be doing, I began to drift back to sleep.

When the wake-up call came, Rick and I slowly floated out of our sleeping bags and quickly brought our focus to the task at hand. The timeline to finish the pre-breathe and get into our suits was filled with countless things to do, and we didn't want to fall behind. I'd long since learned that it was best to get ahead and stay ahead of the timeline.

We spent the next four and a half hours getting into our space suits and depressurizing the airlock to a vacuum. Scott and Tracy helped Rick and me get into our suits and move into position in the airlock. When you're not wearing a space suit, the airlock seems roomy. But two astronauts wearing bulky space suits can quickly make it feel cramped, like sardines in a can. Rick and I floated heads-to-feet. Rick was looking at the airlock hatch, ready to open it when we reached vacuum, while I faced the opposite direction, Rick's feet dangling by my face. In front of me was a panel that we used during the depressurization and repressurization of the airlock.

I carefully went through the process of depressurizing the airlock. Any mistake would result in a delay in opening the hatch and we would be behind on the timeline. *Remember your training and stay focused,* I thought. In space, going slowly to avoid an error is much faster than going fast, making an error, and then having to stop and reconfigure or recover. Everything went smoothly. Cathy's words—"Train like you fly, fly like you train"—echoed in my ears.

"We're ready to open the hatch," I said.

Rick and I had talked about this moment. We knew that we'd be hyperaware of our surroundings when we went outside, and we didn't want to freeze up on a handrail. Would we have a sense of falling like a skydiver when we saw the earth that far beneath us? We'd trained using virtual reality and simulations to prepare ourselves for every eventuality. It was inherently scary entering the cold vacuum of space, but I felt in control.

As I slid out the airlock feet-first, everything was dark. Totally, absolutely dark. The earth was between us and the sun, so there were no lights apart from the ones on our helmets and those of the twinkling cities sprawling beneath us. The helmet on a space suit is fixed, so you can't turn or extend your neck: your field of vision is limited to what's in front of you. I pivoted my body to see if the view changed behind me, but I was surrounded by a deep, infinite blackness that extended in every direction.

Rick had tethered himself to the handrail outside the airlock, and I locked in beside him.

"So much for the view," I said.

"Nothing like opening the hatch during a night pass," Rick replied.

We made our way to the starboard side of the station, and as we reached our next tether station, Tracy radioed us. "Dave, Rick, the sun's about to come up. You can turn off your helmet lights and glove heaters."

I felt the sun before I saw it. My back was to the earth, and I felt myself getting warmer as the station grew brighter around me. It was more than just the sun's warm embrace, though: I sensed its life-giving nature seeping into my suit, as though to say, *Everything is going to be all right.* Before moving on to the next point, I turned to look behind me, and as I saw the spectacular blue of the planet starting to glow, I felt a sense of calm come over me.

We moved to the farthest starboard extent of the station, where we were to install the next major section of the truss on the existing backbone of the station. Rick and I gave feedback to Scorch as he maneuvered the Canadarm2 to bring the new truss into position. It was a delicate handoff—the first Canadian robot arm passing the truss to its successor, and finally from its mechanical hands to our human ones—and once the truss arrived safely, Rick and I got to work.

As Rick and I were tightening the bolts, a drop of water floated up beside my face. *That's odd: there shouldn't be any water in my space suit.* By the time I figured out that the water had come from the mouthpiece of my in-suit drink bag, the drop had adhered to the front of the left lens of my eyeglasses, so I wasn't able to blink it away.

I kept working on the truss as I tried to figure out a solution. I realized that if I angled my forehead forward, I could use the flow of oxygen that came in through the top of my helmet to evaporate the water. No worries: Solve the problem and move on.

After we finished installing the truss, it was time to move the grapple fixture into a permanent stowage location. To get it to there, though, we had to be a bit creative. I stepped into my foot restraint and grabbed hold of the bracket. After we released the bracket, Rick rotated my foot restraint 90 degrees so we could install the piece on the outer side of the station. Once we finished, I was sticking straight out into space.

"Your go for egress," Tracy said over the radio as she watched us from the shuttle's overhead window.

"Copy, my local tether is locked and secure," I said.

On paper, the egress sounded straightforward: I had to release myself from my foot restraint and, while floating in space, reposition myself to turn around and face the outermost portion of the station. Then, using my tether, I would pull myself back in to grab onto the station. But without handrails to pivot my body, it was a tricky maneuver.

I'd practiced this next part dozens of times before, but in that moment everything seemed hyper-real. I pulled on my waist tether, which was attached to my foot restraint, to put force on the bottom of my feet and anchor myself. I slowly rotated one foot out and let it hang beside me. I rotated the other heel and gingerly eased it out of the restraint.

I breathed slowly and tried to block out the thoughts racing through my mind. The space station was moving at about 8 kilometers a second, or 17,500 miles per hour—roughly eight times faster than a bullet—and I was floating freely, with nothing between me and the depths of space except for the tether in my hands.

As I floated there, I looked at the earth far away beneath me. The view was like nothing I had ever seen in my life. Far in the distance were the bright blue waters of the Pacific Ocean with clouds that looked like cotton balls scattered around. Rick and the station were only five feet behind me but they could have been a mile away.

Pull yourself in, Dave, I thought. I gently pulled on the tether to spin and drag myself in toward the station. When I finally locked myself to a handrail, I let out a long, relieved breath. *At least that's the hardest part done.*

Six and a half hours later, Rick and I took once last glimpse at Planet Earth before reentering the airlock on the station. When we finally pulled our helmets off, I turned to Tracy and Scott and said, "Wow, that gets your attention!" In other words, *That was incredible, but I was scared to death the whole time.*

Later that evening I had a chance to call Cathy and the kids. The technology had improved since my first spaceflight, and we could now speak with our families using laptop computers.

"How did it go today?" Cathy asked.

"It was incredible. Scary at points, but amazing."

"How does the planet look from up there?"

"Good question. At first we didn't get to see much, because it was dark when we came out of the airlock. But as we started moving toward the work site, the sun came up and the view was incredible. The tethered egress from my foot restraint was amazing and frightening at the same time."

"I can't wait to hear about it in detail when you get back. Want to talk to the kids?"

"Of course!" There was a scratching over the headset as Cathy passed the phone to Olivia.

"Dad?"

"Hi, Olivia!"

"You sound like you're talking from inside a tin can," Olivia said.

"I kind of am," I said. "But it's a really fancy tin can."

"Are you coming home soon?"

"Not for a few more days, but I'm thinking about you and Evan every day. I love you."

"Love you, too."

They say the second time is always easier than the first. In the case of spacewalking, I'm not so sure, but I'm willing to go with popular belief. Rick and I started the next walk by pulling ourselves hand over hand along the side of the space station. We had to replace a failed gyroscope, a piece of equipment that stabilizes the space station as it orbits the earth, and once again we would have the help of our pilot, Scorch.

The space walk started with Rick and me removing the failed gyroscope and temporarily stowing it by the work site. I then went back to the airlock and stepped into the foot restraint on the end of the Canadarm while Rick continued down to the payload bay. Rick and I would rendezvous in the payload bay to remove the new gyroscope, and I would carry it back to the station while riding the arm.

"I'm in position, Scorch," I said. "You can bring in the arm."

The Canadarm2 swung into view. Of course, you can't just step onto the Canadarm like stepping onto a ladder. I had to attach my tether, then lock myself into the foot restraint on the end of the arm.

I carefully slid my boots under the toe loops and turned my heels outward to lock my boots in place.

"Go for motion," I called to Scorch, and let go of the handrail.

The training arm we'd used underwater at NASA was rigid and jerky, so I was amazed at how smoothly the real thing moved in space. Scorch had to extend me away from the station to reposition me properly over the shuttle payload bay, and as I glided away from the station, I could not help but admire the view.

Behind the shuttle was the curve of the earth, the bright blue of our beautiful planet cast against the black infinite void of space. The oceans were every hue of blue imaginable. I looked past the Canadian flag on my left shoulder to see a pale golden halo surrounding the planet as the sun's rays lit up the atmosphere.

It struck me then: I needed to take a picture of this moment. I reached down to my waist and checked the tether on my camera, then tried to capture the moment with my best point-and-shoot technique. In a space suit, it's impossible to look through a viewfinder, so I just aimed the camera in the direction of the earth and pressed the button, hoping for the best. The camera body was covered with white thermal insulating material, so I wasn't able to see the digital image until after I was back inside the shuttle. *Hope I didn't have my thumb over the lens,* I thought as I put my camera away.

Time seemed to stand still and my mind went back to a movie I had seen in my first year of medical school called *How Can I Not Be Among You?* It celebrated the life of poet Ted Rosenthal. Tragically, Ted was

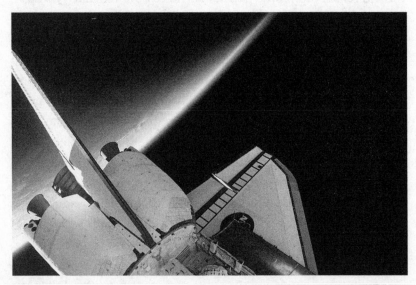

The view of Earth from the Canadarm2 was one of the most spectacular things I've seen in my life. It was truly a moment that lasted a lifetime. *Photo courtesy of NASA*

diagnosed with leukemia in 1970 when he was in his thirties. In his poetry, Ted talked not about the fear of dying but about the fear of living an unfulfilled life. He spoke of the opportunity we all have to live a lifetime in a moment, to savor the moment, to love family, friends, and strangers. Watching the movie was an epiphany for me at the time and has remained so. As soon as the end credits rolled, I promised myself I would live my life to the fullest.

This was one of those moments. I felt connected to humanity. I watched the earth rotate beneath me—a 4.5 billion-year-old planet on which the entire history of the human species, of all living things, had taken place. There were no boundaries visible between countries, simply the majestic beauty of this blue oasis in space. I was in awe and completely humbled. I felt like a speck of sand on an infinite beach. In that moment I realized our legacy is not what we leave, it is how we live. I felt thankful to have had the benefit of Ted's wisdom at such a young age. This was one of many miraculous moments throughout my life, and now, flying in space as a cancer survivor, I was reminded yet again of the importance of living in the moment.

A few minutes later Scorch had me in position over the shuttle payload bay. The gyroscope and its flight support equipment weighed around 1,200 pounds, and I would be holding on to it with two hands, which meant I had to make extra sure I had my feet locked in properly, as they'd be the only thing connecting me to the Canadarm.

"Tethers configured properly?" Tracy called before I asked Scorch to move me straight up out of the payload bay.

"Roger," I responded. Scorch moved me straight up with surgical precision, a testimony to his skill as a robotic operator.

"How's the ride, Dave, and the stability of that big boy?" Scorch asked.

"Great," I said.

Several hours later, after Rick and I had finished installing the equipment, I prepared for my final ride back to the station on the Canadarm. To get me back to the airlock, though, Scorch had to fully extend the arm away from the station, effectively dangling me by my toes into the vast emptiness of space.

"Ready for motion," I said.

"Here we go, Dave," Scorch radioed.

The arm swung out almost sixty feet straight aft of the station. Rick, the station, and everything else disappeared from view. Finally, the arm stopped moving.

"Dave, it'll take me a couple of minutes to reconfigure the arm," Scorch said. "How's the view out there?"

The view in front of me was almost overwhelming. I felt like I was hovering alone in space. It began to feel like I was floating freely; I knew it was an illusion but I still squeezed my eyes shut and repeated to myself, "Heels out, heels out, heels out . . . " reminding myself to lock my feet to hold myself in place.

My heart was pounding, but I cracked my eyes open. The only thing I could see was the earth far away beneath me. The beauty of it was astounding. I slowed my breath and listened to the sound of my own heartbeat. This was the first time I felt completely alone in space. I knew I was still firmly locked into my foot restraint, but I had the sense of floating above the earth, in the heavens, as I watched it go by. We were flying over the Mediterranean, and the white clouds above it rippled into ridges that I felt I could reach out and brush with my hands.

My reverie was interrupted when my radio crackled to life. "Are you ready for motion?" Scorch asked.

The words pulled me back to reality. "Affirmative," I said. I slowly started moving back toward structure, safety, and my crewmates. As I climbed into the airlock feet-first, gently maneuvering around Rick to fit inside, I had one more incredible glimpse of our planet. I grabbed hold of the airlock hatch and paused to appreciate the beauty of the view as long as I could. Every second of it, I knew, would remain with me for the rest of my life.

14

No Such Thing as Normal

After extraordinary experiences, the routine of normal life can almost seem dull. It is easy to long for the rush that comes from an adventure or the thrill of accomplishment, which can sometimes make our day-to-day experiences feel flat by comparison. But the truth is that those moments in between are opportunities to cherish as well. The quiet of the early morning with the smell of a fresh coffee and the sizzling of bacon cooking on the stove; the raw power of a thunderstorm with winds roaring through the trees; the innocence of your infant child falling asleep on your chest—those moments are as important as the others, and if we don't pay attention, it is easy to miss them. Everything can be—and is—extraordinary. Whether it's walking in space or walking down the street, there is so much around us to admire and be thankful for. We just need to find the right way of looking at things.

After I returned from my second spaceflight, I missed the teamwork, the commitment, the need to push myself to be the best that I could be. The end of the mission brought a sense of loss. Once the postflight media events and debriefs were over, we all went our separate ways and took on different assignments. Losing that connection to my crewmates, the people I'd served with for years, left me wondering what was next and whether there was another challenge awaiting me.

"How was work today?" Cathy asked a couple of months after I'd returned from space.

"Our debriefs are mostly done, so we're just waiting to get our new collateral duty assignments."

"That's something to look forward to," she said. "By the way, my schedule has changed a bit, and I'm piloting the redeye to London on Friday. Will you be okay with the kids over the weekend?"

"Of course."

I was looking for any excuse to spend more time with the kids. Now that I was off an active mission, I had more time on my hands, and it gave me a chance to reflect and to delight in their company. So much had happened since I first flew in space, and it was great to enjoy school recitals, weekday family dinners, and reading with them before bedtime.

Cathy and I had agreed before STS-118 that this would be my last mission. The timing was perfect for us to move back to Canada and for Cathy to end her twelve years of commuting back and forth. Retiring also meant opening the door for new Canadian astronauts who would follow me. We started looking for a house in Toronto in late 2007, and I announced my retirement from the space program in February 2008. Cathy and I had talked about it at length, and it seemed like the right decision, but she also knew how hard it was for me.

When we told the kids the news, Evan didn't say anything. He just

Although retiring from being an astronaut meant that I would never again fly in space, I had so much to live for on Earth, including Evan and Olivia.

moved around the table to hug me. He might just be the most huggable person on the planet.

"So you won't be an astronaut anymore?" Olivia asked.

"Technically not," I said.

She frowned as she thought about it. "Good," she said finally.

"Why is that good?" I asked.

"Because now you can just be our dad."

In the months after my retirement was official, I thought about what I might do next. I was only fifty-three: I had lots of life left to live. *Maybe I'll go back to being a doctor,* I thought. I'd always loved the rush of the emergency ward.

One day that spring before the move, it was just Evan and me at home. Cathy was on her way back to Toronto for another flight, and Olivia was over at a friend's house.

"What should we do today?" I asked Evan. He didn't say anything. He just walked over and grabbed a basketball from the closet.

"Great idea," I said as we headed out to the driveway.

Evan dribbled over to the net and threw up a shot. It clanked off the rim and the ball bounced back toward me.

"Nice try," I said. "Give it another shot."

He shot the ball again, this time knocking it off the backboard.

"Almost got it!" I said, passing Evan the ball again.

Evan smiled as he gathered the ball and set up for his next shot. It rolled around the rim, looking like it might go in, only to drop off to the side. Evan raced over to collect the ball and dribbled back to his spot, lining up for another shot.

He took a few more shots, and a few more, and a few more, with only the occasional one scoring. We must have been out there for at least an hour. I kept encouraging him as I collected the rebounds, but after all that time I began to think. *He's trying so hard. Any second now he's going to get discouraged. Maybe he'll feel like a failure. Should I lower the net and make it easier for him?*

I looked at Evan one more time. He held the basketball in both hands. He was beaming, smiling as usual. Suddenly it dawned on me: I was the one with the problem, not him. It wasn't just about the results or accomplishing something—not for Evan. He didn't care at all that the ball wasn't going in. He was perfectly happy practicing and hanging out with his dad—mission accomplished. And there I was, focused on the wrong goal.

Evan launched another shot, and it bounced off the backboard and in.

"Nice!" I said, giving Evan a huge high five. "This is really fun," I said. "I'm having a great time. How about you?" His smile grew even bigger as he answered, "Me, too!"

I watched him shoot for the better part of the next hour, and his glow never dimmed once. It was a great reminder that whatever goals I pursued, the journey was as important as the destination. What mattered was how I felt and what I did along the way. In a world where there is such a focus on outcomes, my special-needs son was showing me that it's what we do on the journey that determines how we reach our destination.

A couple of months after we returned to Canada, I started working at McMaster University and Saint Joseph's Healthcare in Hamilton, where I served as director of a medical robotics program, professor, and health care leader. I loved teaching space physiology and medicine to undergraduate students. Three years later, Southlake Regional Health Centre, a hospital in Newmarket, Ontario, was looking for a new CEO. I took the job because of the incredible staff. They were deeply passionate about patient care, so much so that one time the nurses arranged to bring a patient's horse to the loading dock so they could spend the afternoon together.

Shortly after starting at Southlake, our family life changed again. My nephew, Theo, came to live with us after losing both of his parents to cancer. It was a sad, tumultuous time for our family, but Theo quickly became like one of our own children. Seeing the impact that time had on Theo, I renewed my commitment to live life to the fullest and help him and the rest of my family do the same.

One day I was sitting in my office at Southlake when one of the nurses knocked.

"Sorry to disturb you, Dave, but there's a young boy who's terminally ill who was admitted a couple of days ago," the nurse said. "His dream is to meet an astronaut. Do you think you could help us out?"

"What?" I exclaimed. "It would be my pleasure."

The next day I came into work with my flight suit under my arm. I went up to my office and put the suit on before heading to the elevator. The doors opened and a couple of doctors did a double take as I stepped in.

"Good morning. Nice day, right?" I said.

"What floor?" one of them asked.

"Pediatrics."

When I got to the boy's room, I knocked gently before opening the door.

"Hi there," I said. "I'm Dr. Dave, the astronaut."

Like some kids in palliative care, the boy didn't look as sick as he was. A couple of IVs trailed out from his arms, but he was alert and his eyes lit up when he saw the flight suit.

"So what would you like to know about space?" I asked as I pulled up a chair beside his bed. His parents sat at his bedside, listening attentively.

The boy had all sorts of great questions. We talked for a couple of hours. I described every single detail of the simulations, the flights, the missions. He listened and commented and asked more questions. Time seemed suspended; he wasn't defined by his disease, he was just a curious kid wanting to learn about space and what it would be like to explore. Our time together flew by.

I looked at the boy. "It was really great chatting with you. Your questions were fantastic."

"I just have one more question," the boy said.

"What's that?"

"Do you think I could go to space one day?"

I felt my heart rise to my throat. I struggled to find the right answer. "It is hard to know what will happen in the future," I said. "But what we can do is try and get the most out of each day. With the questions you asked today and what you already know about space, in my mind, you're already an astronaut."

When I got home that night, I was still processing what I'd experienced.

"I met the most remarkable person today," I told Cathy after dinner.

"Who was that?"

"A young boy. He's dying, and he wanted to meet an astronaut. I went to visit him and we talked for hours."

"Sounds like you were able to give him something special."

I teared up a little. "Actually, I think it was the other way around."

I didn't need to explain. Cathy understood.

It's up to us to make the most of every moment.

EPILOGUE

A Lifetime to Go

Our planet is small, our lives are short, but each moment of our lives can last forever if we remember to pay attention. It's easy to feel like the only person in the universe when you're floating in space. But we are never truly alone. Together, we create memories and meaning.

I often think back to my third and final space walk and one particular unforgettable moment when I felt a deep sense of connection—to my teammates in space, to my family, to my friends, and to everyone on the planet beneath me.

Clay Anderson and I were outside the space station. We were tethered to a handrail while flying over the Gulf of Mexico. Houston called us. "Why don't you take a minute and enjoy the view? Hurricane Dean is making its way toward land."

I checked that my tether was securely locked. I released my grip on the handrail to float freely in space. The fans in my suit hummed quietly, the white noise allowing my mind to focus on the awe-inspiring view of our planet. The storm was huge, covering the entire Gulf of Mexico. As we passed over the eye of the storm, I could clearly see the ocean's surface. The hurricane winds were churning the water into choppy waves, but there was perfect calm in the center of the storm. Despite the chaos beneath us, we floated peacefully above in the vast void of space.

Just when I thought it couldn't get any better, the moon rose up over the earth's horizon: night and day, all in one incredible moment. I drank in the view of the great blue planet we call home. I reveled in it.

After a few minutes I slowly made my way back toward the station. Clay went into the airlock first. I entered feet-first beside him and took one final look at the planet beneath me before shutting the airlock hatch behind me. It was hard to come inside.

I knew that would be my last voyage in space. Perhaps that's why the memory is so strong, even now. After I got back to the ground and my career as an astronaut came to a close, I had a choice to make: What was I going to do with the rest of my life? Would I work for myself or for others? All my life, I'd chosen the latter, whether it was working with or leading others at the pool, in the emergency room, or in the space program. And that time was no different. I chose to continue working where I felt I could be most useful: back in health care.

My return to health care reminded me of the importance of serving others and sharing moments with them. I'd seen it before when I was at Sunnybrook. But in that instance it was between a patient and a family member. I was an emergency physician at the time. It was a typical weekend shift, starting off slowly and quickly transforming into the organized chaos that defines the emergency room.

I was just about to sit down for a breather when one of the acute care nurses called. "Dave, you have a new patient that the paramedics just brought in. She's being bagged." This meant that an Ambu bag would be used to help the patient breathe—not a good sign.

I immediately went into the acute care area, where the paramedics were lifting an elderly female patient off their stretcher and onto a hospital bed. I took over ventilating her, but I could tell she was almost gone. I was about to ask the paramedics what happened when I realized that I knew the woman. We'd met when I was a resident rotating in the intensive care unit. She had been admitted with a number of medical issues that ultimately resulted in a diagnosis of amyotrophic lateral sclerosis. ALS is a progressive, untreatable degenerative condition affecting the nervous system. After the woman's initial diagnosis, we discussed many things with her husband and her, including their wishes if she had a life-threatening event. In no uncertain terms, she told me that if anything like that happened, she did not want to be resuscitated.

"My name is Dr. Williams," I said. "Can you hear me?"

The woman gave me an almost imperceptible nod.

"You're at Sunnybrook in the emergency department, and you're having difficulty breathing. What would you like me to do?"

I briefly removed the mask from her face to hear her response.

"Save me," she said quietly.

Her response made absolutely no sense. She had been adamant before about not wanting resuscitation.

She was sliding back into unconsciousness, so I woke her up and repeated the question twice more. Each time, her pale lips gave the same response: "Save me."

Maybe she changed her mind since I last treated her? I thought.

"Does anyone know where her husband is?" I asked.

"Her husband followed us in his car," said one of the paramedics who was writing his report. "He should be here any minute."

I continued manually breathing for the woman for fifteen minutes. Finally her husband arrived. He shuffled into the room as fast as he could with his cane. One of the nurses brought him over to the bedside.

"How is she, Doc?" he asked me. He was short of breath.

"She's unable to breathe on her own," I responded. "I've been helping her breathe. She told me she wants me to save her."

He seemed as perplexed by this information as I was.

I woke her up one more time. "Your husband is here to see you," I said.

She acknowledged me with a slight nod.

"What would you like me to do?" I asked.

Her left hand reached toward her husband. Her husband took it and held it gently in both of his hands. Then she said, "Let me go."

Her husband nodded slowly.

The woman looked only at her husband as I moved the mask away from her face. The gaze from her eyes was one of love for a life partner with whom she'd shared a life's worth of experiences. I pulled the curtains farther around the bed to give them more privacy. As I stepped away, I could hear her husband whispering "I love you" in her ear. Then she drifted away.

It is hard to judge the impact of what physicians do versus what astronauts do. As a doctor, I tried to make a difference to the patients I saw. I tried to help them stay healthy and to maximize their quality of life in any way I could. As an astronaut, I tried to break new frontiers, to make some kind of impact, however small, on the future of human space exploration. Clinicians and researchers will continue to search for new treatments and possible cures for diseases. Astronauts will continue to explore space, going farther and staying longer. The two roles, in the end, aren't so unrelated. In both, I asked myself: Am I doing enough, and am I doing it right?

The experience with the woman and her husband has stuck with me. When I was the CEO of Southlake, one of the projects being considered by the hospital was the construction of a hospice for end-of-life care. It was a complicated, expensive project, and from a strictly business perspective it would have been easy to cancel it. But I'd seen for myself the importance of moments, whether they're total highs like a spaceflight, or well-timed, significant finales like the elderly patient's last moments with her husband. We all deserve to live our lives to the fullest, right up to the end.

With this in mind, I decided this hospice was not a frill but a necessity.

"We need to give people an opportunity to live their final moments to the fullest, surrounded by their loved ones," I told our team.

They agreed.

So we set out to design the perfect environment where families could come together and, despite how hard it is to lose a family member, celebrate old memories and create new ones before the passing of a loved one.

The day the hospice opened, I reflected on how fortunate I have been to live a full life. My mother was a strong supporter of the hospice,

Together with the people who matter most in my life. Left to right: Me, Theo, Olivia, Evan, and Cathy.

but she passed away before it opened. Of all the things I've done in my life, I think this one was closest to her heart. She understood a thing or two about putting others first, both as a nurse and as a mother.

As we completed the hospice, I considered the important people in my life: my parents, Cathy, Evan, Olivia, Theo, my colleagues in space and on the ground. I'd been blessed with a lifetime of shared experiences and explorations, of triumphs and tribulations. So many incredible moments make up a life: diving with my father, learning medicine with my mother, meeting Cathy and our first date in my crappy car, getting married, our two beautiful kids who light up every day, the feeling of weightlessness in space, the joy of working with a team during a mission, the Florida sun on my skin—all lifetimes in themselves.

I considered what the future might bring for me, and I gave thanks that I still had a lifetime to go.

ACKNOWLEDGMENTS

Life presents us with innumerable moments, some we want to remember forever, others we prefer to forget. It is what we choose to do with those moments that determines our happiness, brings contentment, and provides us with meaning in our lives. My life has not always been easy but it has been full; full of wonder, adventure, camaraderie, friendship, family, and love. I would like to thank my amazing wife, Cathy, for thirty-nine years of love, friendship, support, and for being my biggest fan. In many ways, this book is as much a story of our journey together as it is of mine. Thanks for patiently reading the manuscript and for all of your comments and suggestions that helped shape the book from one draft to the next.

To Evan, Olivia, and Theo, watching you grow from childhood into adulthood has been one of the proudest moments of my life. There were times when I felt that parenting was not for the faint of heart, and it is heartwarming to see how things have worked out for each of you.

Thanks, Olivia, for your edits and comments. As a father, one of the most amazing moments is learning from our children and your grace in providing me feedback was greatly appreciated.

Dad, it was tough losing you at such a young age. The last time we chatted was a long time ago, before I was able to achieve the things we had talked about when I was a kid. Thanks for your wisdom, support, and helping me learn the way of the explorer. Mom, you lived to see it all and I was glad to be there to say good-bye. Thanks for sharing your passion for medicine, surgery, and science with me. You inspired me to push through adversity to become a neuroscientist and physician. I will never forget your counsel on the importance of the art of medicine. To my sister, Bronwen, we are very fortunate to have had amazing parents and share lots of great childhood memories.

To my editors, Brendan and Nita, special thanks for your encouragement, support, and patience in helping me put pen to paper (or perhaps fingers to keyboard) to bring some of my stories to life, and for editing the numerous draft versions of the text. To Paul Barker, thanks for the fantastic cover design—it takes me right back to my last space walk. Thanks to the entire Simon & Schuster team for your passion and excitement in helping me publish this book. The journey was incredible and now that we've reached the destination, it will be hard not spending as much time together.

I have had the privilege of participating in two spaceflights and two undersea missions with fantastic teams. To my fellow astronauts and crewmates on STS-90, STS-118, NEEMO-1, NEEMO-7, and NEEMO-9, thanks for some of the most memorable experiences in my life and for your commitment to extending the time-distance constant of human space exploration. It was an honor to be part of the team.

To Roy, Anne, Eve, and Gabriel, thanks for your support and for being such great fans. To friends Bill and Ursula, Laurie and Daniel, Denise and Jim, Jenn and Al, Chris and Helene, thanks for being there for Cathy when I was in space or in the ocean; your friendship has been unwavering. To Brian, flight instructor of the stars and those that go to the stars, thanks for giving me the gift of flight and helping me pass my private pilot license. To the many other flight instructors and instructor pilots I've flown with, thanks for helping me perfect that gift.

To Paul Capelli, George Gate, George Abbey, and Kevin Smith, thanks for helping me be a better leader and giving me responsibilities that enabled me to work with incredible teams. To my teachers Dr. David Harpp, Dr. Ron Chase, Dr. Ken Flegel, Dr. Bruce Rowat, Dr. Lorne Greenspan, and all the other research and clinical teachers who helped me, thanks for making me a better scientist and clinician. To the team at Southlake Regional Health Centre, thanks for tirelessly providing everyone with the ultimate patient experience. To Maggie, Bev, Diana, Tanya, and Tracy, thanks for organizing my life. For the many family members, friends, and colleagues I haven't mentioned, thanks for being part of the journey—it's been an amazing ride.

INDEX

Page numbers in *italics* refer to photographs.